TYSON ISAIAH EVANS

Dear Broken Heart

A 30 Day Guide to Healing Matters of The Heart

Contents

Preface

An Invitation to Heal Together

Many years ago, I made the foolish commitment to never alter the way that I love others, no matter how many times I got hurt. Little did I know the countless trials and tribulations that awaited me on this journey of the heart. It's as if the universe took my declaration as a challenge, whispering, "Oh, my dear, you have no idea what you've just signed up for!"

In the realm of love, I've danced through the delicate balance of vulnerability and resilience, stumbling over heartbreaks and rising from the ashes of shattered dreams. Love has been my greatest teacher, the oracle that speaks in whispers and roars in thunderous echoes. It has shown me the depths of joy and the caverns of sorrow, painting the tapestry of my life with strokes of passion and tenderness.

Oh, I wish I could tell you that this journey has been easy but that would be a delightful falsehood. Love, my dear companions, has a wicked sense of humor. It has tested me in ways I never imagined, throwing me into the chaotic whirlwinds of emotional roller coasters. At times, I found myself laughing hysterically at the sheer absurdity of it all, and at other times, tears streamed down my face as I navigated the intricate maze of the heart.

But midst the trials and tribulations, I discovered a profound truth:

love is both a catalyst for growth and a balm for the soul. It has the power to break us and mend us, to scar us and heal us. Love, my dear friends, is not for the faint of heart. It requires courage, resilience, and a healthy dose of humor to navigate its labyrinthine pathways.

So, here I stand before you, a witness to the tumultuous journey of the heart, armed with tales of triumphs and missteps, of laughter and tears. Through the pages of this book, I invite you to embark on your own odyssey of healing and self-discovery. Together, we shall unravel the mysteries of forgiveness, embrace vulnerability with open arms, and celebrate the power of love in all its glorious messiness.

Maya Angelou once said, "Love recognizes no barriers. It jumps hurdles, leaps fences, penetrates walls to arrive at its destination full of hope." And my dear, we shall leap those hurdles, scale those fences, and crumble those walls that keep us from experiencing the boundless joy and transformative power of love.

So, fasten your seatbelts, my fellow adventurers. Let the journey begin. May these pages be a compass to guide you through the labyrinth of your heart, reminding you that no matter how many times you've been hurt, your capacity to love is an unyielding force that can illuminate even the darkest corners of your soul.

Together, let us embrace the inspiration and laughter that dance hand in hand, for it is in the balance of the two that we find the true essence of our human experience. Let this book be a testament to the resilience of the human spirit and a celebration of the audacity to love, time and time again.

Welcome, to a journey unlike any other. May you find solace, wisdom, and a sprinkle of comedic relief as we embark on this pilgrimage of the heart. Remember, the oracle of love has much to reveal, and it is with open hearts and open minds that we shall receive its divine messages.

I

Embracing the Broken

What you deny or ignore, you delay. What you accept and face, you conquer. - Robert Tew

1

Day 1 Acknowledge The Wound

Have you ever found yourself consistently putting on a façade, pretending that everything is "good" while deep down, you know something isn't right? It's like a lingering headache without a clear cause. We try various temporary fixes—throwing ourselves into fleeting encounters, bouncing from one date to the next, isolating ourselves, immersing ourselves in work, or partying as if there's no tomorrow. But let's get real here: the pain always resurfaces, doesn't it?

Read closely because this is a truth we must confront: the first step towards healing is being brutally honest with ourselves. We must acknowledge and say, "Hey, I'm not okay." And you know what? That acknowledgment is not a sign of weakness; it's a testament to our strength. It takes immense courage to face our own brokenness head-on. I don't share this as a guru or coach, but as someone who has had to intimately confront my wounds face to face in order to emerge beyond the wreckage of heartache. If like me, you have served as leader, healer, or helper to others for the better part of your life, it can be come your system's standard operation to ignore your own sickness while giving medicine to others. However, together we aim to disrupt that system to learn to center the healing of self as our primary goal. So, let's dive deep within and bring to light all the shattered pieces.

When we fully embrace our vulnerable selves, we become less affected by the judgments and rejections of others. The world can be relentless, with people who sway back and forth and circumstances that leave us on shaky ground. However, when we ground ourselves in self-acceptance, we find balance regardless of the obstacles we encounter.

But we won't stop there. Embracing our brokenness is a game-changer. Living in a perpetual state of heartache is like inflicting pain upon ourselves, and that's far from what we deserve. It leads us to believe that we are solely to blame for every ounce of hurt we've experienced. Yes, our own choices can contribute to heartbreak, but that doesn't mean we should punish ourselves indefinitely. Whether it's the pain of a past love or wounds that run deep from our childhood, we carry these broken hearts everywhere, allowing them to dictate our entire lives. They interfere with our friendships, relationships, marriages, and even how we raise our own children. But let me emphasize this, my dear: that's an unjust cycle, not only towards others but primarily towards ourselves.

When we acknowledge our wounds, we take the first step towards healing and reconstructing ourselves from the inside out. As the great Uta Hogen once said, "We must learn to understand and accept the parts of ourselves we'd rather avoid." It's tempting to dismiss negative experiences as mere ups and downs of life. However, if we genuinely confront ourselves, we'll discover emotional wounds, unresolved issues, and psychological barriers that hinder our full potential and strain our relationships.

So, let's rise above and embrace a life without boundaries. Let's commit to acknowledging every fear, insecurity, and worldview that has kept us chained. Whether it's preventing us from pursuing our dreams, experiencing genuine love, or attaining pure wholeness, it's time to break free. You deserve a life that knows no limits, where you can be your authentic and fearless self.

Beautiful souls, lend me your ears and hear this: your journey is unique, but you are not alone. I, too, have faced deep emotional injuries, navigating the painful aftermath of a very public gay marriage and enduring the heart-wrenching process of divorce. But I promise you this: with courage and self-love, you can heal those wounds and release the shackles that hold you back. It won't be a smooth journey, but trust me, it's worth every ounce of effort.

Stay committed to your healing. Remember, it's a process filled with ups and downs. But throughout it all, hold your head high and keep your heart open. Surround yourself with a support system that uplifts and understands you. Seek out communities that celebrate your full identity, where you can share your experiences and learn from others who have walked similar paths.

And let me tell you, there is tremendous power in vulnerability. When you courageously acknowledge your wounds and face them head-on, you are reclaiming your strength and taking control of your narrative. You are no longer defined solely by the pain you've endured, but by the resilience that lies within you. In doing so, you pave the way for a future that is overflowing with self-love, growth, and limitless possibilities.

Now, I won't sugarcoat it and say that this journey will be all rainbows and sunshine. No, my dear ones, there will be moments of messiness.

But I want you to understand that messiness does not equate to failure. It signifies that you are in the process of unearthing layers, peeling back scars, and rediscovering the profound beauty that resides beneath. Embrace every aspect of this journey—the tears, the laughter, and the cathartic moments of self-discovery.

As you continue on this path, you will come to realize that healing is not simply about fixing what is broken. It's about redefining yourself and creating a new narrative—one that is rooted in self-acceptance, self-love, and unapologetic authenticity. It's about embracing the entirety of your journey, celebrating every step of growth, and connecting with your truest self.

Let us embark on this healing journey together. Let us courageously acknowledge our wounds, nurture our spirits, and build a community that celebrates the richness of our unique experiences. We are a collective of resilient souls, powerful beyond measure, and fully deserving of all the love and joy this world has to offer.

Always remember, you are not alone. Your pain is valid, and your healing matters. Together, we will walk this path, supporting and uplifting one another every step of the way. Let us defy the limitations that have been placed upon us, rewrite our stories, and step into the fullness of our divine existence.

Believe in the power of your healing, my dear ones. Trust in the process and know that the journey itself holds tremendous power to heal. Your wounded heart has the capacity to blossom into a wellspring of compassion, wisdom, and profound joy. Stay committed, stay courageous, and embrace the beauty that awaits you on this extraordinary voyage of healing and self-discovery.

Mirror Work Exercise:

Stand in front of the mirror and say, "I embrace my brokenness as a gateway to my healing. I accept all parts of myself, knowing that my brokenness does not define me."

Affirmation:

"I am whole and complete, even in my brokenness. I honor and embrace every aspect of who I am."

2

Day 2 Identify The Source

When we embrace our brokenness, we embark on a journey of self-discovery—a journey that begins with identifying the source. For some of us, this may be a straightforward process. It could be the day we experienced a painful breakup, finalized a divorce, or received news of a loved one's passing. But for others, uncovering the root of our brokenness requires a deeper level of introspection. It's like searching for lost car keys—we must retrace our steps and delve into our past to access the healing we need.

No moment, trauma, encounter, or interaction is too small to be the starting point of our heartbreak. As we dig deep, we may find multiple sources of our pain. It's crucial to confront them head-on, to meet them face to face. It is in these moments of reckoning that we realize the power we have unknowingly granted these sources over our lives.

Take a step back and retrace the path of your development from the very beginning. What unfulfilled longings did you experience in your childhood? Did your family lack time, resources, affection, or stability? It's important to address how our family structure, or the absence thereof, has shaped our worldview. It is during our formative years that we begin to construct emotional walls, and many of our emotional triggers are set. It is an honest assessment to recognize that many of the painful experiences we endure as adults stem from situations that reopen wounds first inflicted in our youth.

The healing process is an ongoing journey of self-evaluation and assessment. We must ask ourselves tough questions: "What am I compensating for?" "What am I trying to prove?" "Why do I care so deeply about this?" or "Why did this particular situation bother me?" By examining our motives and intentions, we can identify the internal voids we are trying to fill and understand their origins.

Identifying the sources of our broken places is not about assigning blame; it's about recognizing the areas of unforgiveness we have held onto. Some of our sources may no longer be present in our lives or have passed away, but in order to experience wholeness in those areas, we must release them. Forgiveness is the act of freeing ourselves from the emotional power that a thing, situation, or individual holds over us. By identifying the sources of our brokenness, we begin to uncover the fragmented pieces of ourselves. This discovery allows us to reconnect those fragments and embark on a journey towards achieving wholeness.

Remember, this process requires gentleness and grace. It's not about dwelling on the pain or dwelling on the past; it's about acknowledging the roots of our brokenness so that we can uproot them and find healing. By bravely confronting our sources of heartbreak, we take a significant step toward reclaiming our power and rewriting our narratives. We open ourselves up to the possibility of reconnecting with our truest selves and experiencing the power of forgiveness.

Loved ones, let us continue this journey of self-discovery and healing. Let us courageously identify the sources of our brokenness, knowing that in doing so, we pave the way for wholeness and restoration. Release the grip of unforgiveness, embrace the fragments of your being, and embark on the remarkable process of reconnecting them. You are worthy of a life lived in fullness, authenticity, and joy. Keep moving forward with grace and resilience, for the path to healing is illuminated by your own inner strength.

Mirror Work Exercise:

Find a quiet and comfortable space where you can sit or stand in front of a mirror. Take a few deep breaths to center yourself and create a sense of calm.

1. Begin by looking into your own eyes in the mirror. Allow yourself to make eye contact with your reflection and acknowledge the person you see before you. Take a moment to appreciate your courage in embarking on this journey of self-discovery and healing.

2. As you gaze at your reflection, imagine that you are peering into the depths of your soul. Visualize yourself retracing the path of your development, from childhood to the present moment. See yourself walking through the significant moments, encounters, and interactions that have shaped you.

3. Focus on the sources of your brokenness that were mentioned in the chapter. Bring to mind any specific moments, traumas, or experiences that come to the surface. Allow yourself to feel any emotions that arise, but remember to approach this exercise with gentleness and self-compassion.

4. With each source of brokenness that you identify, repeat the following affirmations aloud or silently:

- "I acknowledge the sources of my brokenness with compassion and understanding."
- "I release any blame or resentment associated with these sources, freeing myself from their emotional power."
- "I embrace the fragments of my being and embark on a journey of healing and wholeness."
- "I forgive myself for any role I played in perpetuating my own pain or allowing others to hurt me."
- "I am worthy of a life lived in fullness, authenticity, and joy."

1. Take a few moments to reflect on the affirmations and the emotions they evoke within you. Notice any shifts in your perception of the sources of your brokenness and your willingness to release their hold on you.
2. Close the mirror work exercise by expressing gratitude to yourself for engaging in this process of self-discovery and healing. Take a final deep breath and return to the present moment, carrying the intention of continued growth and self-compassion throughout your healing journey.

Remember, mirror work can be a powerful tool for self-reflection and healing. Be patient with yourself as you explore the sources of your brokenness, and always prioritize self-care and self-compassion throughout the process.

3

Day 3 Take Ownership

As we continue our journey towards healing, it's essential that we not only identify the sources of our brokenness but also take ownership of our role in it all. There's an old saying that goes, "when you point one finger, there are four more pointing at you." This step can be challenging because it requires finding a delicate balance between self-blame and personal ownership. It involves two simple statements with profound implications:

Don't take emotional responsibility for anything that you didn't create, and *don't give away emotional responsibility to anyone else for anything that you originated.*

The actions we take as a result of our brokenness are solely our responsibility.

To unpack these concepts, we must face the uncomfortable reality that each of us has habits, idiosyncrasies, proclivities, and traits that contribute to how we are perceived and received by others. While many of these attributes make us unique and wonderful individuals, some may hinder healthy and holistic interactions. For example, if you tend to be jealous and excessively possessive, and a lover rejects that behavior, it's crucial to understand that they are rejecting the behavior, not you as a person. Yet, we might be tempted to internalize their rejection of our negative behavior as a lack of love towards us. In doing so, we make them responsible for our hurt—an understandable but irrational response. Ultimately, regardless of the justification or lack thereof on the part of the "heartbreaker," we cannot allow our hurt to belong to them. The control of our emotions and how we navigate them rests solely on our shoulders. We must own our feelings and take responsibility for the consequences that arise from allowing them to manifest negatively or positively.

When we experience anger, hurt, fear, or other emotions triggered by external or internal factors, we have a choice in how we respond. If we engage in destructive behavior or actions, it's important to recognize that the other person or thing is not to blame, and they will generally not bear the long-term effects of our actions.

It is crucial to make sober emotional decisions and take ownership of them. We have the power to choose how we respond to the circumstances and emotions that arise within us. By accepting this responsibility, we reclaim agency over our lives and pave the way for intentional healing and growth.

Taking ownership does not mean that we dismiss the impact of external factors or absolve others of their accountability. It simply means that we recognize the part we play in our own healing journey. By acknowledging our own contributions to our brokenness, we can begin to break free from patterns of self-sabotage and destructive behavior. It's a courageous step towards self-awareness and self-transformation.

Remember, taking ownership is not an invitation for self-condemnation or blame. It is an opportunity for self-reflection, growth, and empowerment. By embracing our ability to make conscious choices and control our emotional responses, we reclaim our power and become active participants in our healing process.

So, my fellow travelers, let us continue on this path of self-discovery and healing. Let us take ownership of our emotions, actions, and choices, knowing that by doing so, we create space for personal evolution. Choose to respond with intention, love, and empathy. The power to shape our lives lies within us, and through ownership, we unlock the potential for lasting healing and genuine wholeness.

"Heart Check" Journal Prompts:

1. Reflect on a recent situation where you experienced a strong emotional reaction. What were the external triggers and internal factors contributing to your response? Take a moment to identify your role in the situation and how your behavior or actions may have influenced the outcome.

2. Think about a past relationship or encounter where you felt hurt or rejected. In hindsight, what aspects of your behavior or actions may have contributed to the outcome? How can you separate the rejection of your behavior from a personal rejection? Explore ways to take emotional responsibility for your actions and reactions without placing blame on others.

3. Imagine your ideal self, free from patterns of self-sabotage and destructive behavior. What are the characteristics and qualities you would like to embody? How can taking ownership of your emotions and choices help you align with this vision? Set specific

goals or intentions that reflect this transformation and outline steps you can take to work towards them.

4

Day 4 Allow Time For Recuperation

Let's visit the analogy of a broken arm. When we break a limb, we know that there is an incubation period—a time when we must be cautious, avoid overexertion, and allow the limb to heal properly. If we were to continue using the limb as if it were normal, we would risk causing further damage, potentially even permanent harm. I don't have to travel too far to connect with this as I once broke my So why do we treat matters of the heart differently?

I once came across a quote that resonated deeply with me: "To heal a wound, you must stop touching it." The challenge with this concept is that most of us have been conditioned to avoid feeling bad. From the earliest scrape on the knee, authority figures told us to "stop crying." We were taught to mask our emotions and bury our pain. While it is counterproductive to wallow in self-pity, we must learn to be comfortable with allowing ourselves to feel our emotions. Suppressing tears and repressing pain only leads to resentment and unresolved issues. It's important to acknowledge that it's okay to be hurt and to give ourselves permission to mourn our own brokenness. In essence, we need to allow ourselves time to adjust to our heartbreak.

Following any emotional obstacle, whether in the past or present, we must take the time to evaluate how it has impacted our thoughts, outlook, and life expectations. I recall a time when I was engaged and ready to spend the rest of my days with the love of my life. However, faced with infidelity and moral differences, I ended that relationship and quickly moved on without truly addressing the emotional baggage that had accumulated. It wasn't until years later, in my next significant relationship, that I realized the deep-seated trust issues and unresolved emotions that had been lurking within me. As a result, I inadvertently created an environment of confinement for my partner, making them a victim of my past rejection and trust issues.

This pattern is not uncommon. When we fail to take the time to evaluate ourselves and address our unresolved feelings, we subconsciously carry them into new situations. An old issue in a new setting only breeds new issues with familiar outcomes. It becomes a vicious cycle of decisions and consequences that reopen our emotional and psychological wounds from previous heartbreaks. To break free from this cycle, we must interrupt the pattern. Punishing our future for our past is the worst thing we can do.

To interrupt the pattern, we need to press pause after encountering an obstacle and reconnect with ourselves. Take intentional and strategic time to be alone. It could be as little as 15 minutes or longer, but during this time, you are not expected to meet the expectations of others. You don't have to force a smile when you feel like crying. You don't have to be a friend, a sibling, a child, a lover, an employee, an employer, or a parent—just be yourself without pretense. It's a time to unmask and embrace your true emotions. Initially, it may be difficult and painful, but if you persist, you will find it increasingly challenging to remain in that negative space. At the end of your designated time, take a moment to reflect on everything you're grateful for. Dry your tears or re-engage with the world, putting on all the hats and titles you temporarily set aside to enter your personal moment until next time.

There's no definitive measure of how much time you personally need for recuperation, but if you wholeheartedly embrace these moments, you will know when you're ready. In the meantime, resist the urge to rush into anything without evaluating your emotional motives. The reason we need this time for recuperation is to prevent ourselves from making decisions driven by pain. By allowing ourselves to feel the hurt, we regain

control over the subconscious manifestations of our pain, preventing us from making detrimental choices. Instead of becoming a victim by denying our humanity, we prepare ourselves to triumph over our broken hearts.

During this period of recuperation, it's essential to engage in self-reflection and introspection. Take the opportunity to delve deep into your emotions, thoughts, and patterns of behavior. Understand how your heartbreak has influenced your perception of yourself and others. Examine the ways in which it has shaped your beliefs, fears, and expectations. By gaining insight into these aspects, you can begin the evolutionary process of healing and growth.

It's important to note that allowing time for recuperation doesn't mean isolating yourself indefinitely. It's about finding a balance between solitude and healthy connections. Seek support from trusted friends, family, or even professional counselors who can provide guidance and a safe space for you to express yourself. Surround yourself with people who uplift and understand you, allowing you to heal in an environment of love and acceptance.

As you journey through this process, be patient and compassionate with yourself. Healing takes time, and there will be ups and downs along the way. Some days may be filled with immense progress and new-found clarity, while others may feel overwhelming and disheartening. Embrace both the triumphs and the setbacks, knowing that each step forward brings you closer to wholeness.

Remember, healing is not a linear path. It's a messy, nonlinear process that requires courage and resilience. Allow yourself to release the pain, resentment, and bitterness that may have accumulated within you. Forgive yourself and others who may have contributed to your heartbreak. Forgiveness is not condoning the actions or dismissing the pain; it's a powerful act of liberation and self-care. By forgiving, you free yourself from the burden of carrying resentment, and you open up space for true healing to occur.

Throughout this journey, cultivate self-love and self-care as foundational pillars of your recovery. Nurture your physical, emotional, and spiritual well-being. Engage in activities that bring you joy, practice mindfulness and meditation, prioritize restful sleep, and nourish your body with healthy food. Celebrate your progress, no matter how small, and acknowledge the strength and resilience within you.

As you allow time for recuperation, trust that the wounds of your heart will gradually transform into scars—a testament to your resilience and capacity to heal. Embrace the process, knowing that you have the power to rewrite your story and create a future filled with love, joy, and fulfillment.

Tomorrow marks a new day on this journey, where we will explore the importance of our environment. Prepare to embark on a another voyage of self-exploration, where you will uncover hidden strengths, passions, and dreams that will propel you towards a future brimming with possibilities.

Until then, dear broken heart, be gentle with yourself, and know that you are never alone on this path to healing.

Self-Care and Healing Mantra:

I am worthy of healing and self-care. I embrace my brokenness with compassion and understanding. I allow myself to feel my emotions and release any pain or resentment. I am not defined by my past, but I learn from it and grow stronger. I interrupt the patterns that keep me stuck and make choices driven by love and healing. I take intentional time for myself, unmasking and embracing my true emotions. I reflect on gratitude and re-engage with the world, knowing I am resilient. I balance solitude and healthy connections, seeking support from those who uplift and understand me. I am patient and compassionate with myself as I navigate the messy journey of healing. I forgive myself and others, freeing myself from resentment and creating space for true healing. I nurture my physical, emotional, and spiritual well-being with self-love and self-care. I celebrate my progress and acknowledge the strength within me. I trust that my heart's wounds will transform into scars, a testament to my resilience. I am rewriting my story and creating a future filled with love, joy, and fulfillment.

Heart's Healing Blend
Ingredients:

- 1 teaspoon chamomile flowers
- 1 teaspoon rose petals
- 1 teaspoon lavender buds

- 1 teaspoon lemon balm leaves
- 1 teaspoon hibiscus petals

Instructions:

1. Boil 2 cups of water in a kettle or pot.
2. Place all the herbs and petals in a tea infuser or teapot.
3. Pour the boiling water over the herbs and let steep for 5-7 minutes.
4. As the tea steeps, take a moment to inhale the calming aroma and visualize healing energy entering your body.
5. After steeping, strain the tea into your favorite cup or mug.
6. Take a mindful pause, holding the warm cup in your hands and feeling the comfort it provides.
7. Sip the tea slowly, savoring each sip and allowing the healing properties of the herbs to nourish your body and soothe your heart.
8. While drinking the tea, repeat the self-care and healing mantra or any affirmations that resonate with you.
9. Take this time to nourish yourself and embrace the healing power of the tea.
10. Enjoy the moment of peace and serenity that the tea brings, knowing that you are actively supporting your healing journey.

Remember to adjust the recipe according to your personal taste preferences and consult with a healthcare professional if you have any specific medical conditions or concerns.

5

Day 5 Create The Environment

Just as the ill require an incubation period to protect themselves and prevent further exposure to illness, so too do our broken hearts require a healing environment. When we experience heartbreak, it's natural to replay the events repeatedly in our minds, searching for answers and validation. We may even find ourselves drawn to people, places, and things that remind us of our pain, hoping to find solace or justification. But this only perpetuates our suffering.

Amidst the chaos, it becomes paramount to find your place of peace. Whether that be in your faith, the company of trusted friends and family, or engaging in a beloved hobby, stay connected to the sources of tranquility in your life, regardless of the circumstances.

While it's essential to maintain social connections, it's equally important to recognize your limitations. Avoid deliberately placing yourself in situations that will exacerbate your wounds. If your pain stems from a romantic experience, it may be wise to take a step back before fully immersing yourself in the dating world again. If your heartache revolves around your career or purpose, consider giving yourself time before entering environments where your choices might be questioned incessantly. Simply put, take care not to push yourself too far, too fast.

Remember, during your incubation period, it is crucial to prioritize your needs and be intentional about making choices that promote healing and wholeness. You cannot give of yourself if you have nothing left to give. Therefore, an integral aspect of creating a nurturing environment is learning to protect yourself from unhealthy influences. Not everyone deserves access to your vulnerable state. Swiftly identify your allies—those who uplift and edify you—and be strategic about how and with whom you spend your time. Rid your life of toxic people, places, and things that hinder your growth and diminish your sense of self. Cultivate a circle of individuals who provide encouragement, foster personal growth, and contribute to your inner peace. The quality of your environment directly influences the speed at which you heal.

By consciously designing a nurturing environment, you create space for your heart to mend. Surround yourself with positivity, support, and understanding. Allow your healing to unfold in an atmosphere that fosters growth, resilience, and self-discovery. As you provide yourself with the nourishing environment you deserve, you will find that your heart gradually begins to mend and your spirit grows stronger.

Tomorrow, we will explore the significance of self-discovery and the power it holds. Prepare to embark on a journey of self-exploration, where you will rediscover your true essence and uncover the extraordinary potential that resides within you.

Until then, dear broken heart, embrace the healing power of your environment and take solace in knowing that you have the ability to shape your surroundings in ways that nurture your soul.

Tips for Creating a Healing Environment:

1. Find Your Place of Peace: Identify the sources of tranquility in your life, whether it's through faith, spending time with loved ones, or engaging in activities that bring you joy. Stay connected to these sources of peace and make them a priority in your daily life.

2. Recognize Your Limitations: Be aware of your emotional boundaries and avoid situations that may exacerbate your wounds. If you're healing from a romantic experience, take a step back before diving into the dating world again. If your heartache revolves around your career, give yourself time before entering environments where your choices may be questioned. Pace yourself and take care not to push yourself too far, too fast.

3. Prioritize Self-Care: During your healing process, prioritize your needs and make intentional choices that promote healing and wholeness. Take care of yourself physically, emotionally, and spiritually. Nurture your well-being through activities such as exercise, meditation, journaling, or engaging in hobbies that bring you joy.

4. Protect Yourself from Unhealthy Influences: Not everyone deserves access to your vulnerable state. Identify your allies—those who uplift and edify you—and be strategic about how and with whom you spend your time. Remove toxic people, places, and things from your life that hinder your growth and diminish your sense of self. Surround yourself with individuals who provide encouragement, support your personal growth, and contribute to your inner peace.

5. Cultivate a Positive Circle: Surround yourself with positivity, support, and understanding. Create an environment that fosters growth, resilience, and self-discovery. Seek out friends, family,

or support groups who genuinely care about your well-being and understand the importance of your healing journey. Foster relationships that contribute to your inner peace and help you regain your sense of self.

6. Remove Triggers: Identify and minimize triggers that remind you of your pain. This might involve decluttering your physical space, avoiding certain places or activities for a while, or limiting exposure to reminders of the past. Create an environment that supports your healing by removing unnecessary reminders of your heartbreak.

7. Surround Yourself with Inspiration: Fill your surroundings with uplifting and inspiring elements. Decorate your space with meaningful quotes, images, or artwork that resonates with your healing journey. Create a vision board or journal where you can express your dreams and aspirations. Surround yourself with positive affirmations and reminders of your strength and resilience.

8. Create a Calming Atmosphere: Pay attention to the ambiance of your environment. Use soft lighting, soothing colors, and calming scents such as lavender or chamomile to create a peaceful atmosphere. Play relaxing music or nature sounds to promote tranquility. Make your space a sanctuary where you can retreat and find solace.

9. Incorporate Nature: Spend time in nature whenever possible. Surround yourself with natural elements such as plants, flowers, or even a small indoor garden. Take walks in parks or gardens to reconnect with the healing power of the natural world. Nature has a way of grounding us and bringing a sense of peace and serenity.

10. Practice Mindfulness: Cultivate a practice of mindfulness in your environment. Be fully present in the moment and pay attention to your surroundings. Engage your senses and find gratitude in the

small joys of your environment. Practice mindfulness meditation to create a sense of calm and clarity.

Remember, healing is a process, and creating a healing environment is an ongoing journey. Be patient with yourself, make adjustments as needed, and allow your surroundings to support your growth and well-being as you mend your broken heart.

6

Day 6 Believe in Yourself

When we experience rejection or disappointment, we are left feeling angry, devastated, and deeply wounded. In moments of heartbreak, we often lose sight of who we are. Our abilities, appearance, intelligence, and even our purpose come under scrutiny. How is it that the opinions and actions of others can shake us to our core? Why do we turn the blame inward, instead of recognizing that perhaps the situation, person, or circumstance simply wasn't meant for us? The truth is, most of us rely on external validation, whether it's from a partner, friend, career, or position, to affirm our self-worth. This outward-first, inward-second approach is a recipe for disaster. It's time to build the foundation of self-love within yourself, independent of external factors.

Your worth is not dependent on anything other than the fact that you were born—a unique creation crafted in the image of love. You must separate what you do from who you are. You, as an individual, are enough. Everything else is simply an enhancement. Take ownership of your own value. You set the standard for how the world perceives you. In the realm of public relations, perception is everything. Treat yourself as your own brand, and present yourself accordingly.

Many failed relationships stem from the mistake of placing the responsibility for our happiness on our significant other. True partnership and happiness can only be achieved when you are content in your own skin. Contrary to popular belief, and conventional math, two halves don't make a whole when it comes to matters of the heart. Don't give anyone or anything outside of yourself the power to define your happiness or value. They will inevitably fall short, not because of their shortcomings, but because no one else can truly understand what it takes to make you feel wholly valued and loved. If you live from a place of self-worth and self-love, others will have no choice but to see it. Those who genuinely desire to contribute to your happiness will simply reflect and match the love and value they witness within you. By nurturing your own self-love, you create a protective shield against the blows that life may bring.

Embrace a lifestyle of self-validation. Take yourself on dates, dress up just because, and treat yourself with kindness. The deeper your appreciation for the person you are, the easier it becomes to appreciate others and for others to appreciate you. When you have the ability to validate your own love, you become impervious to the approval of others. By proving your worth to yourself, you no longer rely on anyone else's validation.

Believe in yourself, dear broken heart. Cultivate a love and appreciation for who you are. By doing so, you will gain the strength to weather any storm and face any challenge that comes your way. Tomorrow, we will explore the transformative power of forgiveness and how it can liberate your heart from the shackles of pain. Get ready to embark on a journey of healing and freedom as you learn to forgive yourself and others.

Remember, you are worthy of love and happiness, simply because you exist. Embrace your unique essence and let your self-love radiate outwards, lighting the path towards a brighter, more empowered future.

Mirror Work Exercise:

Mirror work is a powerful tool for building self-love and reinforcing your worthiness. This exercise will help you embrace your unique essence and cultivate a deep appreciation for yourself. Find a quiet space and a mirror where you can practice this exercise:

1. Stand or sit comfortably in front of the mirror, ensuring that you can see your reflection clearly.
2. Take a few deep breaths to center yourself and bring your attention to the present moment.
3. Gently gaze into your own eyes and let your reflection become a symbol of self-acceptance and love.
4. Repeat the following affirmations to yourself, looking directly into your own eyes:

- "I am worthy of love and happiness simply because I exist."
- "I separate what I do from who I am. I am enough as I am."
- "I take ownership of my own value and set the standard for how the world perceives me."
- "I am content in my own skin, and my happiness comes from within."
- "I embrace a lifestyle of self-validation and treat myself with kindness and appreciation."
- "I am impervious to the approval of others because I validate my own love and worth."
- "I believe in myself and my abilities. I have the strength to overcome any challenge."

1. As you repeat each affirmation, let the words sink in and feel their truth within you. Allow yourself to fully embrace the love and acceptance that they represent.
2. Take a moment to reflect on the person you see in the mirror and appreciate the unique essence that you bring to the world. Recognize your strengths, talents, and the beauty of your soul.
3. Express gratitude to yourself for taking the time to cultivate self-love and for embracing your worthiness.
4. Whenever you need a reminder of your self-worth, return to this mirror work exercise and repeat these affirmations. Let them serve as a daily practice of self-empowerment and love.

Affirmation:

"I am worthy of love and happiness simply because I exist. I separate what I do from who I am, knowing that I am enough as I am. I take ownership of my own value and set the standard for how the world perceives me. I am content in my own skin, finding happiness within myself. I embrace a lifestyle of self-validation and treat myself with kindness and appreciation. I am impervious to the approval of others because I validate my own love and worth. I believe in myself and my abilities. I have the strength to overcome any challenge. I am deserving of love, joy, and fulfillment."

7

Day 7 Open Your Eyes

As we embark on a journey of self-acceptance, our vision becomes clearer. Embracing our own brokenness goes beyond personal healing—it also involves recognizing the pain and brokenness in others. Often, what keeps us down after experiencing heartache is the mistaken belief that we suffer alone in our despair. It can feel like the rest of the world is celebrating while we're left in the shadows. Failing to acknowledge the suffering of others in relation to our own pain can lead to resentment and a pattern of victimhood.

When we're in the midst of our own pain, the last thing we want to hear is that someone else has been through similar struggles or that others have it worse. These reminders, however, are essential to our healing. Building a bridge to our own healing requires connecting with the pain and healing journeys of others. Having the ability to discern the pain of another person empowers us with a sense of community and the hope that we are not alone in our suffering. When we find the strength to compassionately contribute to the healing of others, we gain a broader perspective on the scope of our own heartbreak.

By opening our eyes to the hurt and brokenness around us, we become less sensitive to the actions of those who have caused us pain. Instead of taking offense, we must recognize that most of the hurtful things people do are a result of their own brokenness. Broken hearts often lead to dysfunctional behaviors. It's crucial for us to look beyond the surface and understand the underlying symptoms of dysfunction. This doesn't mean we should allow others to mistreat us without consequences, but developing an empathetic perspective helps us build healthy boundaries and protects us from experiencing heartbreak as a result of someone else's negative manifestations of dysfunction.

As you continue on this journey of healing, let your eyes be open to the pain and brokenness in others. Extend compassion and understanding, knowing that we are all on this imperfect journey together. By embracing awareness, you gain a greater capacity for empathy and resilience.

II

Facing Our Dysfunction

"I have found that battling despair does not mean closing my eyes to the enormity of the tasks of effecting change, nor ignoring the strength and the barbarity of the forces aligned against us. It means teaching, surviving and fighting with the most important resource I have, myself, and taking joy in that battle. It means, for me, recognizing the enemy outside and the enemy within, and knowing that my work is part of our power. "

Audre Lorde

8

Day 8 Identify Your Dysfunction

When our bodies experience illness, they activate their natural defense mechanisms, deploying white blood cells and other fighter cells to combat foreign invaders and minimize damage. Similarly, the immune system of our hearts, symbolizing the core of our souls, operates in a similar manner. With each disappointment, trauma, or heartbreak, our hearts develop defense mechanisms to protect us from further harm. However, these defense mechanisms can sometimes become excessive. Just as leukemia begins with an overproduction of white blood cells that attack healthy functions in the body, our heart's defense system can overproduce dysfunctions that disrupt the natural patterns of our soul and heart.

We are inherently wired to love and possess a capacity for forgiveness, as exemplified by children. Two kids can have a spat on the playground, swear never to be friends again, call each other names, and yet be best friends again by the end of recess. However, as we grow older, life tends to diminish our ability or willingness to reconcile and forgive. Instead, we often transform perfectly healthy intrinsic characteristics into unhealthy defense mechanisms that help us cope with our broken hearts, blocking out both positive and negative opportunities.

In my opinion, there are about five basic archetypes of the broken-hearted. Take a moment to see if any of these resonate with you:

The Recluse:
   The Recluse is the loner among us. They prefer solitude and spend most of their time alone. They believe that being alone minimizes their exposure to potential heartbreak. They have crafted the defense of shutting others out.

The Social Butterfly:
   This archetype hides their emotional pain through excessive social-ization. They are always surrounded by a crowd and often become the life of the party. The Social Butterfly thrives in this environment because it provides a false sense of validation, allowing them to avoid the true healing that begins with solitude.

The Workaholic:
   This individual uses their career and excessive busyness as an emotional shield. They convince themselves that they simply don't have time for emotions. As long as they remain consumed with work, they can avoid addressing their inner selves.

The Sex Siren:
   To shield themselves from further emotional damage and create a sense of validation, this type relies on attraction and sexuality. They often avoid commitment in favor of "freedom." By leveraging sex appeal, they gain a false sense of empowerment.

The Brick Wall:

This person allows no one to get close. People may share with them, but they remain guarded about their own emotions. Their feelings are locked away in a vault, with the key hidden. Indifference is often their preferred coping mechanism.

While these archetypes of brokenness may vary, they all thrive on two common elements: avoidance and defense. We adopt these behaviors in an attempt to evade our pain and shield ourselves from further suffering. It is crucial that we identify our defense mechanisms and, most importantly, detach the belief that these dysfunctions define who we are. We must uncover our shells and shields before we can begin to shed them.

To identify and address our dysfunctions, we need to embark on a journey of self-reflection and introspection. It requires a willingness to confront our pain and examine the ways in which we have built walls to protect ourselves. By acknowledging these defense mechanisms, we can start the process of dismantling them and fostering true healing.

It's important to remember that these dysfunctions are not inherent aspects of our identity. They are adaptations we have developed in response to our past hurts and disappointments. They may have served a purpose at some point, but now they hinder our growth and prevent us from experiencing true connection and fulfillment.

To begin the process of identifying our dysfunctions, we can engage in a Mirror Work exercise:

Find a quiet and comfortable space where you can be alone with your thoughts.

Look into a mirror and make eye contact with yourself. Take a few deep breaths to center yourself.

Start by affirming your worth and acknowledging that you are ready to confront your dysfunctions and release them.

Reflect on the archetypes mentioned earlier—the Recluse, the Social Butterfly, the Workaholic, the Sex Siren, and the Brick Wall. Which one resonates with you the most? Are there elements of multiple archetypes that you can relate to?

Take a moment to observe any patterns or behaviors that align with your chosen archetype. How do these behaviors manifest in your life? How do they affect your relationships, personal growth, and overall well-being?

With compassion and self-forgiveness, recognize that these dysfunctions are not serving you in a healthy way. They may have provided temporary protection, but they no longer serve your highest good.

Affirm your commitment to release these dysfunctions and open yourself up to healthier ways of relating to others and yourself. Repeat a positive affirmation such as: "I am willing to let go of my dysfunctions and embrace a healthier way of being. I am open to healing and growth."

Take a few moments to journal about your reflections and insights. Write down any action steps you can take to start dismantling your dysfunctions and creating positive change in your life.

Remember, this journey of self-discovery and healing takes time and patience. Be gentle with yourself as you navigate through the layers of your emotions and past experiences. By identifying and releasing your dysfunctions, you create space for authentic connection, personal transformation, and a more fulfilling life.

Affirmation:

"I am ready to identify and release my dysfunctions. I embrace the process of healing and growth. I am deserving of healthy relationships and genuine connection. I am open to new possibilities and ready to step into my truest self."

9

Day 9 Find Your Patterns, Unraveling the Cycle

Have you ever felt like no matter what you do, you keep finding yourself in the same situations? It's as if you're stuck in a loop, experiencing failed relationships, career setbacks, or recurring emotional cycles. Despite your best efforts, you can't seem to break free from the patterns that hold you back. This is because humans are creatures of habit by nature, and our dysfunctions have created behavioral patterns that keep us trapped. It's time to uncover and understand these patterns to pave the way for true transformation.

Our emotional patterns are born from triggers and reactions. When someone or something strikes a chord within us, reminding us of a past negative experience, we instinctively react based on coping mechanisms we developed or behaviors we adopted to avoid repeating the pain. These patterns are often unintentional and ingrained within us.

For example, let's say your supervisor at work unknowingly does something that triggers a negative memory from a previous job. As a result, you find yourself reacting by becoming less productive, withdrawing into yourself. This pattern can be summarized as follows: Catalyst + Reaction = Withdrawal. Understanding these patterns is a crucial step in the active and intentional process of healing.

To uncover your patterns, you must make a conscious effort to be aware of your responses to people and situations when faced with negative experiences. Take the time to reflect on how you react, what triggers your emotions, and the behaviors that follow. By becoming cognizant of these patterns, you gain valuable insight into your own psyche.

However, it's equally important to examine the patterns that lead you to these negative experiences in the first place. If you've been repeatedly fired from multiple jobs or experienced infidelity in multiple relationships, it's time to evaluate the commonalities. Ask yourself questions such as: What similarities do these partners share? What initially drew me to them? Why did I choose this job? Was it out of necessity alone? Embrace this critical self-evaluation with courage and honesty.

Before you can dismantle detrimental patterns, you must first identify them through a thorough evaluation process. This self-reflection and exploration will help you gain clarity on the choices you make and the patterns that have shaped your life. It is through this understanding that you can break free from the repetitive cycles and make room for positive change.

Remember, this process takes time and patience. Be gentle with yourself as you delve into the depths of your patterns and experiences. By unraveling the cycle and finding your patterns, you empower yourself to rewrite your story, create healthier habits, and embrace a future filled with purpose and fulfillment.

Affirmation:

"I am ready to break free from my limiting patterns. Through self-awareness and introspection, I gain clarity on the choices I make. I release old behaviors that no longer serve me, and I embrace new patterns that align with my growth and well-being. I am the author of my own story, and I am creating a future filled with joy and fulfillment."

Mirror Exercise - Breaking Free from Patterns

Take a moment to find a quiet space where you can be alone with your thoughts. Stand in front of a mirror and look into your own eyes. Take a deep breath and let it out slowly, allowing any tension to melt away.

As you gaze into the mirror, reflect on the patterns in your life that you want to break free from. It could be patterns in relationships, career choices, emotional reactions, or any other recurring themes that hold you back. Acknowledge that these patterns have played a role in your journey but affirm that you are ready to move beyond them.

Now, focus on one specific pattern that you want to unravel. Visualize it as a tangled knot, representing the cycle that keeps repeating. As you continue to gaze into the mirror, imagine yourself holding a pair of golden scissors. These scissors symbolize your power and determination to cut through the pattern and break free.

Take a deep breath and repeat the following affirmation aloud or in your mind:

"I am ready to break free from this pattern that no longer serves me. With clarity and self-awareness, I am empowered to make different choices. I release the old and embrace the new. I am the author of my own story, and I create a future filled with purpose and growth."

As you recite the affirmation, visualize yourself confidently cutting through the tangled knot with the golden scissors. Feel a sense of liberation and lightness as the pattern dissolves before your eyes.

Take a moment to reflect on how it feels to let go of this pattern. Notice the freedom and possibility that opens up when you release what no longer serves you. Embrace the empowerment that comes with breaking free and creating new, healthier patterns in your life.

Finish the mirror exercise by thanking yourself for the courage to confront your patterns and commit to personal growth. Take a final deep breath, exhaling any remaining tension or doubt.

Carry this sense of empowerment with you throughout your day, knowing that you have the ability to break free from old patterns and embrace a future filled with positive change. Trust in your own strength and resilience as you continue to unravel the cycles that no longer serve you.

10

Day 10 Break Free from Patterns

Armed with the knowledge and recognition of our patterns, we now embark on the journey of breaking free from them. These patterns have become deeply ingrained within us over a considerable period of time, so it may require some effort and determination to dismantle them. It's one thing to be aware of our patterns, but it's an entirely different challenge to consistently recognize when we are engaging them. We must bring these patterns to the forefront of our consciousness and be able to say to ourselves, "I'm doing it again."

Similar to someone trying to quit smoking, finding an alternative behavior is essential. Unless we are robots, we will have emotional reactions to various stimuli. It's crucial to intentionally replace detrimental reactions with positive and opposite responses. This may involve adopting a new hobby, incorporating a different workout routine, or engaging in prayer and meditation. Once we have identified the triggers, we can use meditation as a tool to redirect our attention and distract ourselves in triggering situations.

Remember, practice makes new habits. If we consistently replace our negative reactions to negative emotional stimuli with positive responses, we will gradually build up a resistance. Over time, things that once bothered us will begin to lose their power over us. Breaking these simple yet deeply rooted emotional patterns has the potential to transform our lifestyle. It liberates us to view things from an experiential standpoint rather than being confined by our historical lens.

By breaking free from our patterns, we create space to explore deeper levels of self and others. We no longer allow our patterns to limit our capacity to embrace new experiences. Each day, we strive to build healthier habits and develop responses that reflect a healed state of being. Just as in the wild, wounded and fearful creatures can be the most dangerous, our negative patterns can hinder our ability to build relationships and achieve our goals. Therefore, we must consciously invite positive experiences into our lives by intentionally creating positive habits.

As we embark on this journey of breaking free from patterns, let us embrace the transformative power of our choices. Each step forward brings us closer to a life filled with abundance, growth, and fulfillment. Let us release the grip of old patterns and open ourselves to the boundless possibilities that await us. With every positive habit we cultivate, we create a brighter future for ourselves and those around us.

Breaking free from patterns requires a commitment to self-awareness and intentional change. It's not a one-time event but a continuous process of growth and evolution. As you embark on this transformative journey, remember to be patient and compassionate with yourself. Breaking patterns takes time, effort, and persistence.

One powerful strategy is to surround yourself with a supportive community. Seek out individuals who are also on a path of personal growth and who can hold you accountable. Share your intentions with them and invite them to offer guidance and encouragement along the way. Together, you can celebrate your progress and navigate the challenges that may arise.

Additionally, it's important to reframe your mindset. Instead of seeing patterns as restrictive or limiting, view them as opportunities for growth and self-discovery. Each pattern you break is a step towards greater freedom and authenticity. Embrace the belief that you have the power to create a new narrative for your life, one that is aligned with your true desires and values.

During this process, be mindful of the triggers that lead you back into old patterns. Identify the situations, people, or thoughts that tend to activate your default reactions. By recognizing these triggers, you can develop strategies to respond differently. This might involve taking a pause before reacting, practicing deep breathing techniques, or reframing negative thoughts into more empowering ones.

As you break free from patterns, celebrate your victories, no matter how small they may seem. Acknowledge the progress you've made and the strength it took to choose a different path. Remember that change is not always linear, and setbacks are a natural part of the process. Embrace them as opportunities to learn and adjust your approach moving forward.

Above all, trust in your ability to create a new reality for yourself. Believe that you are deserving of a life filled with joy, love, and abundance. As you continue to break free from patterns, you will discover a sense of empowerment and liberation that will permeate every aspect of your being.

Today, make a conscious decision to break free from the patterns that no longer serve you. Embrace the uncertainty and embrace the unknown. Step boldly into the realm of possibility, knowing that you have the power to shape your own destiny. The journey may be challenging at times, but the rewards are immeasurable.

You are capable. You are resilient. You are ready to break free and create the life you truly deserve. Trust in yourself, trust in the process, and trust in the infinite possibilities that await you.

In order to solidify your commitment to breaking patterns, it can be helpful to create daily affirmations that reinforce your intentions. Affirmations are powerful statements that align your thoughts and beliefs with the positive changes you want to manifest in your life.

Repeat these affirmations daily, preferably in front of a mirror, and speak them with conviction and belief:

I am aware of my patterns, and I have the power to break free from them.

I release old patterns that no longer serve my growth and well-being.

I embrace change and invite new experiences into my life.

I am open to learning and evolving from my past experiences.

I choose empowering thoughts and responses that align with my true self.

I release fear and step into a future filled with love, joy, and abundance.

Each day, I am creating new, positive habits that support my growth and happiness.

I am worthy of a life free from limiting patterns and full of limitless possibilities.

I am resilient, and I trust in my ability to navigate through challenges and create positive change.

I celebrate my progress, no matter how small, and I am grateful for the journey of self-discovery.

As you speak these affirmations, visualize yourself breaking free from old patterns and stepping into a new, empowered version of yourself. Embrace the emotions and sensations that arise as you connect with these affirmations, allowing them to deeply resonate within you.

In addition to affirmations, incorporate mirror work into your daily routine. Stand in front of a mirror, look into your eyes, and speak words of love, encouragement, and empowerment to yourself. Affirm your worthiness, acknowledge your growth, and express gratitude for the strength and resilience you possess. Mirror work helps to deepen your connection with yourself and reinforces a positive self-image.

Remember, breaking patterns is a journey of self-discovery and transformation. It requires dedication, self-reflection, and a willingness to step outside of your comfort zone. Be gentle with yourself during this process and celebrate every milestone along the way. You have the power to break free and create a life that reflects your true essence. Embrace the opportunity to rewrite your story and embrace the limitless possibilities that await you.

11

Day 11 Adjust Your Expectations Of Yourself

Growing up in my family, there were high expectations placed upon me. I was constantly reminded to be the "golden child," to excel academically, achieve greatness, surpass the achievements of those who came before me, and make everyone proud. These expectations became a burden, leading me to set unrealistic and unattainable standards for myself. I know many of you can relate to this experience. For some, it may have been the opposite, where people expected so little of you that you felt the need to prove them wrong and pushed yourself to exhaustion to outperform even your best efforts. Whether it's excessive expectations or underestimation, both ends of the spectrum can leave us feeling broken.

Our personal expectations of ourselves often inflict the deepest wounds. We look around and compare ourselves to others, falling into the trap of the "grass is greener" effect. We dwell on the plans and aspirations our younger selves had for our future, only to be faced with the stark reality of the disparity between our expectations and our current reality. Standing in front of the mirror, we scrutinize our bodies, noticing the perceived flaws and feeling like there are missing pieces in our lives. All of us have areas where we feel we have fallen short of our own expectations. However, dwelling on these self-imposed disappointments does not lead to action or promote healing. By fixating on what we expected ourselves to do or be, we rob ourselves of the potential for growth and transformation. Let's admit it: despite our various perfectionist tendencies and relentless efforts, we are imperfect, flawed, and beautifully human.

The great news is that every day we wake up, we are given the opportunity for reinvention. Instead of wallowing in the void of unfulfilled personal expectations, let's embrace the chance for self-development. Regardless of how difficult it may be, we must come to terms with who we are in this very moment. The counterproductivity of maintaining unrealistic expectations for ourselves is insurmountable. We often turn minor setbacks into towering mountains of disappointment. And once that mountain has been erected, serving as a memorial to our regrets, it becomes a trap that immobilizes us, preventing us from taking action.

In simple terms, it's time to let go of what we thought should have been!

Each day is an opportunity for self-improvement, one step at a time. False expectations only create limitations. Instead, set goals, have desires, and work towards them without the weight of your own expectations dragging you down. Find freedom in your achievements by allowing yourself to embrace your limitations and imperfections.

On the other hand, it's important to recognize that until you try, you have no idea what you are truly capable of achieving. Some of us need to adjust our negative expectations of ourselves. Banish the word "can't" from your vocabulary. Adjusting your expectations is a twofold process.

It involves letting go of the limited mindset of "should've been, would've been, could've been" and embracing the infinite possibilities of "can be."

It's time to break free from the chains of unrealistic expectations and embrace the journey of self-discovery and growth. Give yourself permission to make mistakes, learn, and evolve. You are capable of so much more than you realize. Adjusting your expectations opens up a world of infinite potential and allows you to embrace the beauty of who you are in this very moment. Let go of the past, release the weight of expectations, and step into the realm of endless possibilities.

Mirror Exercise:

Stand in front of a mirror and take a deep breath.

Look into your own eyes and acknowledge the expectations you have placed upon yourself.

Reflect on the ways these expectations have weighed you down and limited your growth.

Repeat the affirmation below while maintaining eye contact with yourself:

Affirmation:

"I release unrealistic expectations and embrace my authentic self. I am imperfect, yet beautifully human. I let go of what should have been and embrace the infinite possibilities of what can be. I adjust my expectations and open myself to the journey of self-discovery and growth. I am free to make mistakes, learn, and evolve. Each day is an opportunity for reinvention. I accept and love myself just as I am in this moment. I am capable of achieving greatness by embracing my true potential. I am resilient, empowered, and ready to embrace the endless possibilities that await me."

Take a moment to appreciate your reflection and internalize the affirmations.

Carry the affirmation throughout your day, reminding yourself of your inherent worth and the power of adjusting your expectations.

12

Day 12 Adjust Your Expectations of Others

As we journey through life, we encounter numerous individuals who play significant roles in our personal narratives. We often develop expectations of how these people should behave, how they should respond to us, and how they should reciprocate our actions. Yet, more often than not, these expectations lead us down a path of disappointment and heartache. It is crucial for our own emotional well-being and the health of our relationships to adjust our expectations of others.

From a young age, we have an inherent trust in people and a belief that they will live up to our ideals. However, as we grow older, we realize that even the most well-intentioned individuals can fall short of our expectations. We make the mistake of assuming that others will respond and act as we would in a given situation. But the truth is, everyone has their own unique perspectives, experiences, and ways of navigating the world.

To free ourselves from constant disappointment, we must make two profound shifts in our perspective:

Don't expect people to respond as you do: Each person has their own set of values, beliefs, and ways of processing emotions. What may seem like a natural response to us may not be the same for someone else. Holding others to our personal standards only sets us up for frustration and resentment. Instead, let us approach interactions with an open mind, embracing the diversity of human behavior and understanding that everyone has their own journey.

Reciprocity is not common: It is natural to desire reciprocity in relationships, expecting that if we give something, we will receive something in return. However, this expectation can lead to disappointment when others don't meet our perceived standards of reciprocity. We must shift our mindset and understand that people have their own reasons for their actions or lack thereof. Acts of kindness and love should stem from a genuine place within us, not as a transaction for future rewards.

Disappointment often arises from unfulfilled expectations based on assumptions we make about others. We may assume that people will act in a certain way because of their relationship to us or our past experiences with them. However, these assumptions can be destructive to healthy and trusting relationships. It is essential to hold others accountable for what they explicitly say they will do, but it is equally important not to hold them accountable for what we assume they should do.

Communication plays a vital role in managing expectations. Instead of presuming that others know what we need or expect from them, we must actively educate them about our love languages, preferences, and boundaries. By openly expressing our needs, we provide others with the opportunity to understand and support us better. It is unfair to hold people accountable for expectations we have never made clear to them.

Another significant source of disappointment is the expectation of reciprocity. We may find ourselves giving selflessly, only to feel let down when we don't receive the same level of care or attention in return. However, we must shift our mindset and realize that genuine acts of love and kindness should be given without the expectation of something in return. When we attach expectations to our expressions of love, we become conditional in our affections, which goes against the essence of our character.

By learning to give and do without expectations, we not only reduce our disappointment but also open ourselves to unexpected rewards and blessings. Our acts of love should come from a place of authenticity and selflessness, allowing us to maintain our character regardless of how others respond. Embracing this mindset allows us to experience the true essence of love and builds stronger and more fulfilling connections.

So, let us adjust our expectations of others. Let us embrace the uniqueness of individuals and recognize that their responses may differ from ours. Let us communicate our needs and boundaries, providing others with the opportunity to support us better.

Affirmation:

"I release my expectations of others and embrace their unique journeys. I allow love and understanding to guide my interactions, knowing that everyone has their own perspective and way of being. I give without attachment and receive with gratitude, understanding that true connections are built on authenticity, not expectations."

Mirror Work Exercise:

Find a quiet and comfortable space where you can be alone with your thoughts.

Stand in front of a mirror and take a few deep breaths to center yourself.

Look into your own eyes in the mirror and repeat the following affirmations:

"I release the need to control or change others. I accept them as they are, with their own strengths and weaknesses."

"I let go of expectations and allow space for understanding and compassion in my relationships."

"I communicate my needs and boundaries clearly, giving others the opportunity to support me."

"I give love and kindness freely, without attaching expectations or conditions."

"I am worthy of love and respect, regardless of how others respond or behave."

As you repeat each affirmation, observe your emotions and any resistance that arises. Allow yourself to acknowledge any past disappointments or frustrations related to unmet expectations.

Take a moment to reflect on how adjusting your expectations can lead to greater freedom, understanding, and healthier relationships. Visualize yourself interacting with others from a place of love, acceptance, and authenticity.

Close the mirror exercise by expressing gratitude for the opportunity to grow and adjust your expectations. Take a final deep breath, and carry the affirmations and insights with you throughout your day.

Remember, this mirror work exercise is a journey of self-reflection and growth. Repeat it regularly to reinforce the positive mindset and reinforce the practice of adjusting expectations for your own well-being and the health of your relationships.

13

Day 13 Open Your Mind: Embracing Possibilities

Our past experiences, heartbreaks, and dysfunctions have a profound impact on our thought processes. They shape the way we perceive the world and limit our beliefs about what is possible for our future. To truly find fulfillment and wholeness, we must break free from the confines of our past and open our minds to new possibilities. In this chapter, we will explore the importance of regaining an open mental capacity, embracing change, and expanding our horizons.

Our past pain and disappointments create a lens through which we view the world. We confine ourselves to what we have already felt, done, or experienced, limiting our potential for growth and happiness. It is crucial to recognize that the future holds endless possibilities, irrespective of our past. By opening our minds to the idea of happiness, wholeness, and fulfillment, we create space for new opportunities and transformative experiences.

As we journey through life, we develop preferences and attractions based on our past encounters. However, these preferences can become limiting if we cling to them too tightly. We must be willing to expand our scope of what we like, what we believe we are worth, and what our life can be. Just because we have always enjoyed certain things or followed certain patterns doesn't mean we should confine ourselves to them. Embracing new experiences and possibilities enriches our lives and opens doors to unexplored avenues of joy and growth.

Many people find comfort in familiarity and tend to stick to what they know. However, this familiarity can become a barrier to true fulfillment. Our comfort zones may provide temporary solace, but they limit our potential for growth and discovery. To break free from the confinements of our comfort zones, we must allow our minds to be open to new possibilities. It's about stepping outside the candy-coated confinement and venturing into the unknown with a sense of curiosity and excitement.

Open-mindedness is not about rejecting our past or dismissing our favorite experiences. It's about expanding our repertoire of likes and embracing change as a natural part of life. By cultivating an open mind, we invite new perspectives, opportunities, and relationships into our lives. We challenge ourselves to grow, evolve, and adapt to the ever-changing circumstances. It is through openness that we find fulfillment, purpose, and a deeper connection to ourselves and the world around us.

By opening our minds to new possibilities, we break free from the limitations imposed by our past and embrace a future filled with fulfillment and joy. It is essential to let go of the shackles of familiarity, expand our scope of life, and remain receptive to change. As we navigate our journey with childlike wonder and the wisdom gained from our experiences, we discover that our possibilities are truly endless. So, take a leap of faith, open your mind to the vastness of life, and allow yourself to embrace the beautiful unknown that awaits you.

Affirmation:

"I am open to the endless possibilities of life. I release the limitations of my past and embrace the new experiences and opportunities that come my way. My mind is receptive to change, growth, and fulfillment. I welcome the unknown with curiosity and excitement, knowing that it holds the potential for my greatest joy and transformation."

Mirror Exercise:

Stand in front of a mirror and take a few deep breaths to center yourself.

Look into your own eyes and affirm, "I am ready to open my mind to new possibilities."

Reflect on any limiting beliefs or patterns that have held you back in the past. Acknowledge them without judgment.

Now, visualize yourself breaking free from those limitations, as if stepping out of a confining box.

Repeat the affirmation, feeling the words resonate within you: "I am open to the endless possibilities of life."

Take a few moments to imagine the vastness of opportunities that lie ahead. See yourself embracing change, trying new things, and expanding your horizons.

As you continue to gaze into the mirror, express gratitude for the journey that has brought you to this point and for the growth that awaits you.

End the exercise by reaffirming your commitment to staying open-minded and embracing the beautiful unknown that life has in store for you.

Throughout your day, whenever you encounter resistance or doubt, repeat the affirmation to yourself as a reminder of your willingness to embrace new possibilities.

14

Day 14 Relinquish Resentment: Embracing Healing and Freedom

Imagine holding lit fireworks in a sealed box. What would happen? The fireworks would undoubtedly ignite and explode, fulfilling their purpose. However, the box itself would also suffer, burnt and damaged. This analogy captures the destructive nature of resentment. Resentment, characterized by bitter indignation at perceived unfair treatment, may stem from valid reasons, but it is a cancerous disease that corrodes our compassion, clouds our judgment, and breeds self-pity. To facilitate healing, it is crucial that we release the grip of resentment, both towards others and ourselves.

One of the most irrational aspects of resentment is that it often targets individuals or situations that have no cognitive awareness of the unfairness we perceive or the hurt we experience. It is a burden we carry, poisoning our own well-being while the other party remains oblivious. Recognizing this, we are faced with two choices: address the issue or let it go. While neither option may initially seem enticing, they hold more promise for our personal growth than holding onto resentment ever will. Resentment, if left unchecked, festers into bitterness, contaminating our interactions, mindsets, and overall outlook on life.

If we opt to address the resentment, it is crucial to assess its justification before engaging in a conversation with the other person involved. While justification is not a prerequisite for initiating the conversation, it does shape our approach. Furthermore, we must brace ourselves for potential opposition. When confronting the source of our resentment, it is essential to understand that our primary objective is to express and release, not to control the other person's response. Our healing should be the focal point, the ultimate prize. Stay focused on that goal.

It is important to acknowledge the intricate link between resentment, trust, and expectations. By reassessing and adjusting our expectations, we may discover that the foundation of our resentment is unfounded and irrational. As individuals on the path to wholeness, we must shed all emotional paradigms and mechanisms that no longer serve us or contribute to our ability to serve others. Resentment serves no purpose, offers no benefits, and cannot undo the actions that triggered it. Regardless of the method chosen to relinquish resentment, it is crucial to make a conscious effort to free ourselves from its grip. The consequences of holding onto resentment are far too great, and there are no rewards to be gained from it. It is time to let it go and embrace healing and freedom.

Affirmation:

I release all resentment and embrace a life of freedom and peace. I choose to let go of past hurts and open my heart to love and compassion. I am worthy of healing and growth.

Mirror Exercise:

Find a quiet space where you can be alone and look into a mirror. Take a few deep breaths to center yourself and bring your focus to the present moment. As you gaze into your own eyes, repeat the following affirmations:

"I acknowledge any feelings of resentment that I have been holding onto."

"I understand that resentment does not serve me and it is time to release it."

"I choose to forgive myself and others for past hurts."

"I let go of the weight of resentment and embrace a life of freedom and peace."

"I am open to healing, growth, and genuine connections."

"I deserve to live a life filled with love, compassion, and joy."

"I am worthy of happiness and fulfillment."

Take a few moments to reflect on each affirmation, allowing the words to sink in and resonate within you. As you continue the mirror exercise, visualize the resentment dissolving and being replaced by a sense of lightness and inner peace. Smile at yourself in the mirror, expressing love and acceptance towards the person you see.

III

Shifting Your Perspective

"A shift in perspective opens a completely new set of unlimited possibilities."
Satsuki Shibuya

15

Day 15 Embrace Your Worth

From an early age, we learn that the things we are denied often hold a certain allure and fascination. While this tenacity can fuel our determination, it can also lead to an unhealthy addiction to rejection. As we pursue our deepest desires, we encounter disappointments and setbacks, which can create a distrust of success and a disdain for what comes easily. The truth is, many of us are drawn to what seems unattainable. However, this mindset hinders our journey towards wholeness and healing, requiring us to intentionally reframe our perspectives on desire.

It is essential to recognize that our natural inclinations are not always aligned with our happiness or well-being. Reconditioning ourselves does not mean giving up the thrill of the chase or the excitement of pursuing our dreams or relationships. Instead, we must value our own interests in a way that ensures alignment with our worth. We need to be aware of our motivations for being attracted to someone or something, ensuring they are congruent with our values and growth.

Many of our desires are formed as a response to abundance or deprivation in our past. If we grew up in a structured environment, we might crave freedom and spontaneity. If we witnessed weakness, we might seek strength. However, pursuing the extreme opposite of what we are trying to escape can disrupt balanced relationships and a balanced life. Achieving wholeness and healing requires recognizing and halting trivial pursuits that lead us astray. We deserve fruitful and prosperous relationships that nurture our well-being.

When we long for emotionally unavailable or aloof individuals, it is not others rejecting us but rather ourselves rejecting our worth. If we do manage to attain our elusive target, we validate ourselves conditionally. If we fail, we use the experience to berate our self-esteem. These self-inflicted brushes with rejection perpetuate a cycle that only reinforces our need for validation. Instead of changing our attractions, we embark on an even more heart-wrenching journey.

The belief that there are no good men or women out there, or that pursuing our dreams is pointless, does not reflect reality but rather our inability to value virtues over reckless and detrimental patterns. Instead, we must operate from a lens of self-worth. We are deserving of love, choice, and fighting for what truly matters. We are a priority in our own lives. Choosing acceptance means walking through positive doors when they open, giving genuinely kind and persistent individuals a chance, and putting rejection in its rightful place.

Affirmation:
I embrace my worth and reject the cycle of rejection. I am deserving of love, fulfillment, and prosperity. I release the need for validation from unhealthy pursuits. I choose to pursue what aligns with my values and growth. I am open to healthy relationships and opportunities. I am confident in my worthiness and choose acceptance in all aspects of my life.

Mirror Exercise: Stand before a mirror in a calm and private space.

Take a few moments to center yourself and bring your focus to the present. Look into your own eyes and repeat the following affirmations:

1. "I acknowledge any patterns of seeking rejection in my life."
2. "I release the need for validation from unhealthy pursuits."
3. "I am deserving of love, fulfillment, and prosperity."
4. "I embrace my worth and choose to pursue what aligns with my values and growth."
5. "I am open to healthy relationships and opportunities that nurture my well-being."
6. "I am confident in my worthiness and choose acceptance in all aspects of my life."

Reflect on each affirmation, allowing the words to resonate within you

16

Day 16 Push Past Persona

One of the greatest things I've ever done for myself was to allow myself to change even if it contradicts previous notions of "Who I am". In our journey towards healing and wholeness, we often find ourselves wearing masks and adopting false personas as a means of coping with life's challenges. These self-images, created to protect us, can become barriers to our true authenticity. The ego self and imposter syndrome take center stage, inhibiting our ability to fully embrace who we are. To reach a place of genuine wholeness, we must embark on a process of shedding these false identities and inviting true authentic living into our lives.

Throughout our lives, we accumulate various false self-images that we present to the world. These personas may be born out of societal expectations, past traumas, or the need for acceptance and validation. We become so accustomed to wearing these masks that we forget who we truly are at the core. The weight of these false identities burdens our souls, leading to feelings of disconnection, emptiness, and an underlying fear of being exposed as a fraud.

At the heart of these false self-images lies the ego self and the imposter syndrome. The ego self is the voice within us that seeks external validation and constantly compares ourselves to others. It thrives on maintaining the illusion of control and perfection, often at the expense of our true selves. On the other hand, imposter syndrome whispers doubts into our ears, making us believe that we are undeserving of our accomplishments and that we will eventually be exposed as frauds.

To break free from the shackles of false self-images and embrace authentic living, we must take deliberate steps towards self-discovery and self-acceptance. These steps include:

Awareness: Recognize and acknowledge the masks you have been wearing and the false identities you have adopted. Reflect on how they have influenced your thoughts, behaviors, and relationships.

Self-Reflection: Engage in deep introspection to uncover your true desires, passions, and values. Reflect on the moments in life when you felt most alive and authentic. Explore your strengths, weaknesses, and areas for growth.

Embracing Imperfections: Understand that perfection is an unattainable ideal. Embrace your imperfections as unique aspects of your being. Allow yourself to be vulnerable and release the fear of judgment.

Authenticity in Action: Take small steps towards aligning your actions with your true self. Express your thoughts, opinions, and emotions authentically. Surround yourself with people who value and support your genuine self.

Self-Compassion: Practice self-compassion and kindness throughout this shedding process. Understand that it takes time and patience to unlearn ingrained patterns and embrace authenticity. Be gentle with yourself as you navigate this journey.

As you shed the layers of false self-images, you create space for true authentic living. Embrace the freedom of being your genuine self, unencumbered by societal expectations or the need for external validation. Trust in your unique qualities and the value you bring to the world. Celebrate your authenticity and allow it to permeate every aspect of your life.

Shedding false self-images is a courageous and transformative journey towards healing and wholeness. By recognizing the influence of the ego self and imposter syndrome, and taking deliberate steps towards embracing authenticity, we invite true joy, fulfillment, and genuine connections into our lives. Let go of the masks, push past persona, and embark on the path of true authentic living, where your true self can shine brightly for all to see.

Affirmation:

"I release the false self-images and masks that no longer serve me. I embrace my authentic self and live in alignment with my true desires and values. I am worthy of love, acceptance, and success simply by being my genuine self. I let go of the need for external validation and trust in my unique qualities and strengths. I celebrate my authenticity and allow it to shine brightly in every aspect of my life. I am courageous, resilient, and deserving of a life filled with joy, fulfillment, and genuine connections."

Mirror Work Exercise:

Mirror work is a powerful tool for shedding false self-images and embracing authenticity. Find a quiet space and a mirror where you can practice this exercise:

1. Stand or sit comfortably in front of the mirror, ensuring that you can see your reflection clearly.
2. Take a few deep breaths to center yourself and bring your attention to the present moment.
3. Gently gaze into your own eyes and let your reflection become a symbol of self-acceptance and authenticity.
4. Repeat the following affirmation to yourself, looking directly into your own eyes:
5. "I release the false self-images and masks that no longer serve me. I embrace my authentic self and live in alignment with my true desires and values. I am worthy of love, acceptance, and success simply by being my genuine self. I let go of the need for external validation and trust in my unique qualities and strengths. I celebrate my authenticity and allow it to shine brightly in every aspect of my life. I am courageous, resilient, and deserving of a life filled with joy, fulfillment, and genuine connections."
6. As you repeat the affirmation, let the words sink in and feel their truth within you. Allow yourself to fully embrace your authentic self and release any attachment to false identities.
7. Take a moment to reflect on the person you see in the mirror and appreciate the courage it takes to shed the masks and embrace authenticity. Recognize your true desires, values, and the beauty of your genuine self.
8. Express gratitude to yourself for taking the time to cultivate self-acceptance and embrace authenticity.
9. Whenever you need a reminder of your authentic self, return to this mirror work exercise and repeat the affirmation. Let it serve as a daily practice of self-empowerment and authenticity.

17

Day 17 Tell The Truth: Embracing Radical Authenticity

Throughout our lives, we have become masters of crafting facades and presenting false versions of ourselves. We do this to shield ourselves from the judgments and consequences of others. This habit of telling white lies and half-truths starts in childhood and carries over into our adult interactions. To truly progress on the path of healing, we must shed the masks of inauthenticity in all their forms. Day 17 is dedicated to embracing radical authenticity and the transformative power of telling the truth.

Presenting a false self not only perpetuates the cycle of brokenness, but it also creates a breeding ground for disappointment and shattered expectations. When we invest time and effort into shaping how others perceive us, we set ourselves up for inevitable failure. The things or people we acquire as a result of this false self are built on shaky foundations. Eventually, they either leave us or undergo significant changes. We interpret these outcomes as abandonment, when in reality, it is the rejection of the lie we have been living.

To break free from the cycle of brokenness, we must choose radical authenticity. This means embracing the truth in all aspects of our lives, both internally and externally. Here are some key steps to help you on this transformative journey:

Radical Honesty with Self: Take a courageous look within and confront the lies you have been telling yourself. Recognize the patterns of inauthenticity and acknowledge the fears and insecurities that have driven them. Embrace radical honesty about your desires, dreams, and shortcomings.

Practice radical honesty in your interactions with others. Speak your truth without fear of judgment or rejection. Share your thoughts, feelings, and experiences openly and authentically. Be willing to have difficult conversations and express your true self, even if it feels uncomfortable at first.

Release the need for others to validate your truth. Understand that not everyone will accept or understand your truth, and that is okay. Focus on attracting people who appreciate and embrace your authenticity, rather than building relationships on false pretenses.

Embracing Vulnerability: Allow yourself to be vulnerable and transparent, even when it feels uncomfortable. Share your struggles, fears, and insecurities with trusted individuals who create a safe space for you to express yourself authentically. Embracing vulnerability opens the door to deeper connections and genuine understanding.

Living in Freedom and Joy: As you continue to embrace radical authenticity, you will experience a newfound sense of freedom. Living in truth liberates you from the shackles of pretending and allows you to fully embrace who you are. This freedom becomes the foundation for lasting joy and fulfillment.

Telling the truth and embracing radical authenticity is a transformative journey that leads to genuine healing and wholeness. By shedding the masks of inauthenticity and living in truth, we break free from the cycle of brokenness and create space for meaningful connections and lasting joy. Choose to live in the freedom of truth and embrace radical authenticity as you continue on your journey towards wholeness.

Affirmation:

I am shedding false self-images and embracing my authentic self. I release the need to conform to others' expectations. I am worthy of love and acceptance just as I am. I choose to live authentically and wholeheartedly.

Mirror Exercise:

Find a quiet space where you can be alone with your thoughts.

Stand in front of a mirror and take a deep breath.

Look into your own eyes and allow yourself to see beyond the surface.

Repeat the following affirmations aloud or in your mind, with conviction and sincerity:

"I release the need to wear masks and pretend to be someone I'm not."

"I acknowledge my true desires, dreams, and insecurities without judgment."

"I embrace my authentic self and let go of the fear of rejection."

"I am deserving of love and acceptance just as I am."

"I choose to live in radical authenticity and invite true and authentic living into my life."

Take a moment to reflect on any emotions or insights that arise during this exercise.

End the exercise by expressing gratitude for your journey towards authenticity and self-discovery.

18

Day 18 Accept Your Worth

In a world that constantly tries to define our value based on external measures, it is crucial that we take a stand and unapologetically accept our worth. Society bombards us with messages that seek to diminish our self-esteem and convince us that our value is contingent upon achievements, possessions, or the approval of others. But deep within us, there lies an unwavering truth: we are inherently valuable, just as we are.

Accepting our worth begins with a radical shift in our mindset. We must reject the notion that our value is tied to external validation or societal standards. Our worth is not determined by our appearance, our accomplishments, or the opinions of others. It is an inherent quality that exists within us, simply because we are alive.

Owning our worth means recognizing and honoring our unique strengths, talents, and qualities. It means celebrating our individuality and embracing the truth that we are enough, exactly as we are. We don't need to prove ourselves or seek validation from others to validate our worthiness. We are worthy by birthright.

When we fully accept our worth, it permeates every aspect of our lives. It influences the choices we make, the relationships we engage in, and the way we show up in the world. We no longer settle for less than we deserve or tolerate mistreatment. We set boundaries that protect and honor our inherent worth, and we surround ourselves with people who uplift and celebrate us.

Accepting our worth also means taking responsibility for our own self-care and well-being. We prioritize our physical, mental, and emotional health because we recognize that we are deserving of love, care, and nourishment. We make choices that align with our values and honor our authentic selves.

In a world that often tries to diminish our worth, it takes courage to stand tall and accept our inherent value. But when we do, we create a ripple effect of empowerment and inspire others to do the same. We become beacons of self-acceptance and self-love, igniting a revolution of embracing worthiness in all its forms.

Today, I choose to accept my worth unconditionally. I release the need for external validation and embrace the truth that I am inherently valuable. I celebrate my unique qualities and honor my authentic self. I make choices that align with my worth and surround myself with love, respect, and positivity. I am deserving of all the good that life has to offer, and I step into my power as a person of worth.

Take a moment to reflect on your inherent worth. Recognize the qualities that make you unique and valuable. Embrace your worth unconditionally and affirm your commitment to living a life that honors your inherent value.

Affirmation:

I am inherently valuable and worthy, simply because I exist. My worth is not defined by external measures or the opinions of others. I embrace my unique strengths, talents, and qualities with love and acceptance. I honor my authentic self and make choices that align with my inherent worth. I deserve to be treated with respect, kindness, and love. I am worthy of all the good that life has to offer. Today and every day, I fully accept my worth.

Mirror Exercise:

Find a quiet and comfortable space where you can be alone with your thoughts. Stand in front of a mirror and take a few deep breaths to center yourself. Look into your own eyes in the mirror and take a moment to connect with your inner self.

Repeat the following affirmations while maintaining eye contact with yourself:

"I am inherently valuable and worthy."

"I embrace my unique strengths, talents, and qualities."

"I honor my authentic self and make choices that align with my worth."

"I deserve love, respect, and kindness."

"I am deserving of all the good that life has to offer."

Take a few moments to reflect on these affirmations and allow their truth to sink in.

Smile at yourself in the mirror, acknowledging the strength and courage it takes to accept your worth.

End the exercise by expressing gratitude for the person you see in the mirror and the inherent worth that resides within you.

IV

Making Healthy Choices

"One thing we can do is make the choice to view the world in a healthy way. We can choose to see the world as safe with only moments of danger rather than seeing the world as dangerous with only moments of safety."
Deepak Chopra

19

Day 19 Eat to Heal: Nourishing Body, Mind, and Spirit

The concept of "you are what you eat" holds a deeper truth when it comes to our journey of healing and wholeness. What we choose to intake - be it food, information, or entertainment - plays a significant role in shaping our well-being. In order to align ourselves with the path of healing, we must be intentional about what we allow into our bodies, our minds, and our spirits. It's time to eat like we agree with our healing.

Let's start with the physical aspect of eating. Many of us have an emotional relationship with food. In times of pain, stress, or other emotional triggers, we may find ourselves overindulging or depriving ourselves. However, these extremes are detrimental to our well-being. Physical health is closely intertwined with emotional health, and by making conscious choices about what we eat, we can positively impact our overall balance and self-esteem. When we fuel our bodies with a balanced and nourishing diet, we often find that our emotional state improves, and we feel better from the inside out.

But eating to heal goes beyond just the physical realm. It extends to the spiritual and mental aspects of our lives as well. Just as we carefully select our food, we must also be mindful of what we feed our minds and spirits. This includes the books we read, the music we listen to, and the media we consume. If we are going through a difficult emotional period, subjecting ourselves to content that amplifies bitterness or heartbreak may hinder our healing process. It's important to surround ourselves with positivity, empowerment, and reflections that propel us forward on our journey towards wholeness.

Eating to heal doesn't mean completely abstaining from the foods, music, or entertainment that we love. It's about finding a balance and recognizing when something no longer serves our overall well-being. Food should not be a crutch, and our entertainment choices should not consume us in unbridled emotionalism that perpetuates dysfunction. We are more than just physical beings; we are spiritual beings as well. It's essential to feed ourselves with things that promote the health of both our spirit and body.

So, as we embark on this path of healing, let us be mindful of what we choose to intake. Let us nourish ourselves with wholesome and nourishing foods, positive and empowering thoughts, and uplifting and inspiring content. By being intentional about what we eat, think, and consume, we are taking a significant step towards aligning ourselves with our healing and embracing a life of wholeness.

Affirmation for Day 19:

I choose to eat to heal and nourish my body, mind, and spirit. I am mindful of what I allow into my life, making conscious choices that promote my overall well-being. I am in control of what I intake, and I align myself with the path of healing and wholeness.

Mirror Exercise for Day 19:

Take a moment to stand in front of a mirror, looking into your own eyes with love and acceptance. Repeat the following statements aloud, allowing them to resonate deeply within you:

I am worthy of nourishment in every aspect of my being - body, mind, and spirit.

I acknowledge the power of my choices and the impact they have on my well-being.

I release any emotional attachment to food, embracing a balanced and nourishing diet that supports my physical and emotional health.

I am selective about the information and entertainment I allow into my life, choosing content that uplifts and empowers me.

I honor my worth by surrounding myself with positivity, inspiration, and reflections that align with my journey of healing and wholeness.

Each day, I make intentional choices to eat, think, and consume in a way that promotes my overall well-being.

I embrace the transformative power of nourishment, knowing that as I eat to heal, I am nourishing my body, mind, and spirit.

20

Day 20 Stop The Search, Embrace Your Inner Power

On this journey of healing, there comes a pivotal moment when we must make a powerful choice—to stop searching outside of ourselves for what we already possess within. It's easy to believe that we need something or someone to complete us, whether it's love, a special connection, or a missing piece of our lives. However, the truth is that everything we truly need resides within us. Our outer circumstances are mere reflections of our inner state.

It is imperative that we learn to release the notion of lacking and seeking external validation. Instead, we must redirect our focus inward, discovering the vast reservoirs of love, joy, and strength that already exist within our being. The healing process requires us to reclaim our power and take full responsibility for our own wholeness. We are the ultimate creators and fillers of the voids we feel, and the solutions lie within our own hearts and minds.

Continuing the search for fulfillment outside of ourselves only perpetuates our sense of brokenness. Others cannot bear the weight of our stability or provide the permanence we seek. Spouses, partners, careers, children, or achievements are not meant to be the foundation of our wholeness, but rather beautiful additions that enhance the already solid infrastructure we create through our choice to embrace our broken places, confront our dysfunctions, shift our perspectives, and actively choose healing.

The key lies in recognizing that we possess an innate power to generate love, joy, peace, and fulfillment from within. We can become our own source of stability and happiness. By embracing our vulnerabilities, acknowledging our past wounds, and committing to self-love and self-care, we tap into an unlimited wellspring of strength and wholeness.

So, today, I encourage you to stop the relentless search for external validation and instead turn your gaze inward. Affirm that within you lies the power to heal, to love, and to find true joy. Embrace the responsibility for your own growth and well-being. Choose to release the victimhood of your brokenness and step into the role of the empowered creator of your own destiny.

You are enough. You possess everything you need to live a life of purpose and fulfillment. Trust in your own inner wisdom and embrace the incredible power that resides within you. It's time to stop searching and start embracing the abundant possibilities that await you on the path of self-discovery and healing.

21

Day 21 Choose Peace, Embracing Serenity Within

In the midst of life's chaos and constant demands, it is crucial to remember that peace is not merely a distant ideal but a choice we can actively make in every moment. Day by day, we have the power to cultivate a state of inner serenity, regardless of external circumstances. Today, I invite you to embark on a journey of choosing peace as a way of life.

Peace is not the absence of conflict or the absence of challenges. It is the ability to remain centered and calm amid the storms that inevitably come our way. It is a conscious decision to detach from chaos and embrace a state of inner tranquility. This choice is not always easy, but it is essential for our overall well-being and healing.

To choose peace, we must first recognize the factors that disturb our inner equilibrium. These may include negative thoughts, past traumas, unhealthy relationships, or self-sabotaging behaviors. It is important to confront these sources of unrest with courage and self-compassion. Healing requires us to address the root causes of our pain and actively work towards resolution and growth.

Once we have identified the factors that disrupt our peace, we can take intentional steps to mitigate their impact. This may involve setting boundaries with toxic individuals, seeking professional help to heal emotional wounds, or adopting practices that promote mental and emotional well-being, such as meditation, journaling, or therapy. Each of us has unique needs and preferences, so it's important to find what works best for us individually.

Choosing peace also requires us to release the need for control and surrender to the flow of life. Often, our distress arises from trying to manipulate outcomes or clinging tightly to expectations. However, true peace comes when we trust in the divine timing of the universe and surrender our desires to a higher power. It is in this surrender that we find freedom from anxiety and an opening for miracles to occur.

In the pursuit of peace, radical self-acceptance plays a vital role. Embracing our flaws, imperfections, and past mistakes allows us to let go of self-judgment and cultivate self-compassion. We must remember that we are human beings on a journey of growth and learning. Embracing our inherent worth and acknowledging our progress along the way empowers us to choose peace over self-criticism.

Mirror Work Affirmation:

"I choose peace as the guiding force in my life. I release all that disturbs my inner tranquility and embrace serenity within. I surrender my need for control and trust in the divine timing of the universe. I am worthy of love, compassion, and peace. Today, I choose to let go of self-judgment and accept myself fully. I am deserving of a life filled with peace and joy."

As you go about your day, remind yourself of this affirmation. When faced with challenges or moments of unrest, take a deep breath and consciously choose peace. Embody the serenity that lies within you and let it radiate out into the world. Remember, peace is not something to be found externally—it is a choice we make within ourselves, and it has the power to transform our lives.

22

Day 22 Choose Balance

In our fast-paced and demanding world, it is easy to lose sight of the importance of balance. We often find ourselves caught up in the whirlwind of responsibilities, obligations, and expectations, neglecting our own well-being in the process. However, today marks a pivotal moment in our healing journey—the day we consciously choose to bring balance back into our lives.

Balance is the art of harmonizing the various aspects of our existence: mind, body, and spirit. It is the recognition that our well-being depends on nurturing all facets of our being equally. Just as a tightrope walker must find equilibrium to stay steady, we too must find equilibrium in our lives to thrive.

To choose balance, we must first assess the areas of our lives that have become imbalanced. Are we neglecting our physical health while pouring all our energy into work? Are we sacrificing our relationships for personal ambitions? Are we neglecting our spiritual well-being in pursuit of material gains? It is crucial to identify these areas and acknowledge the need for change.

Once we have identified the imbalances, we can take deliberate steps to restore equilibrium. This may involve setting boundaries in our work life, prioritizing self-care and rest, fostering meaningful connections with loved ones, or dedicating time to activities that nourish our soul. Balance is not a one-size-fits-all concept—it requires us to align our actions with our unique needs and values.

Choosing balance also means recognizing that we cannot do it all or be everything to everyone. It requires us to let go of perfectionism and the unrealistic expectations we place upon ourselves. It means accepting that it is okay to say no, to delegate tasks, and to ask for help when needed. By releasing the need to control every aspect of our lives, we create space for balance to flourish.

In the pursuit of balance, self-awareness is a powerful tool. We must continuously check in with ourselves, listening to the whispers of our body, mind, and spirit. Pay attention to the signs of stress, exhaustion, or dissatisfaction. Engage in practices such as meditation, journaling, or simply quiet contemplation to gain clarity on what areas of your life are in need of adjustment.

Today, I invite you to stand before the mirror and affirm your commitment to choosing balance:

"I choose balance as the guiding principle of my life. I acknowledge the areas of my life that have become imbalanced and commit to restoring equilibrium. I prioritize self-care, nurturing relationships, and tending to my spiritual well-being. I release the need for perfection and embrace the power of saying no. I am aware of my own needs and honor them. Today, I choose to live a life of harmony and balance."

As you go about your day, remember this affirmation. Take small steps towards bringing balance into your life. Seek moments of stillness and reflection, making intentional choices that support your overall well-being. Remember, balance is not an end goal but a continuous practice—an ongoing dance of adjustment and recalibration. By choosing balance, you create the foundation for a fulfilled and harmonious life.

23

Day 23 Think Affirmatively

In the grand tapestry of life, our thoughts weave the threads that shape our reality. Whether you call it faith, the law of attraction, or simply the power of positive thinking, the ancient wisdom that our thoughts have the ability to manifest our desires remains true. Just as God spoke, "Let there be light," and created the universe, we too possess the creative power within our thoughts. Today, we embark on a journey to think affirmatively and unleash the immense potential of our minds.

Our thoughts are the architects of our lives, laying the foundation upon which our dreams are built. It is crucial to choose our thoughts with utmost care, focusing on the affirmative rather than dwelling on the possibility of failure. Often, we find ourselves conditioned to anticipate the worst-case scenarios, allowing doubts and fears to overshadow our desires. However, we must shift our mental energy towards envisioning the results we wish to achieve.

Controlling our thoughts is a delicate and intricate skill, one that requires dedicated practice. We must train ourselves to redirect our focus from the obstacles that stand in our way to the outcomes we seek.

What we focus on, we manifest. Each thought is a seed planted in the fertile soil of our consciousness. If we sow seeds of negativity, fear, and doubt, we will reap a harvest abundant in negativity, fear, and doubt. Instead, let us craft our expectations and desires from a place of inner knowing, empowered by the belief that we have the ability to receive what we truly desire.

It is essential to recognize that our mindset and perspective shape the majority of our life's achievements. The external circumstances, the actions done to us or for us, hold far less influence than the power of our own thoughts. When we consciously choose to think in the affirmative, we seize control of our future and destiny to the best of our human capabilities. Consider the example of salespeople—two individuals armed with the same tools and product. The difference in their mental approach determines their outcomes. One hopes to avoid rejection, while the other expects success. Two mindsets, two distinct results.

No matter how many times we have experienced failure or setbacks, we must choose relentless belief. Make daily affirmations of what you want to see manifested in your life. Create vision boards adorned with images that represent your desires. Affirm those desires, walk in alignment with those affirmations, and witness the transformation as your dreams begin to take shape. Over time, the reality you hoped for becomes your lived experience.

Today, I encourage you to stand before the mirror and affirm your commitment to think affirmatively:

"I choose to harness the power of my thoughts. I release doubts and fears, embracing the belief that my desires are within reach. I shift my mental energy towards envisioning the outcomes I seek. I am the architect of my own reality, and my thoughts shape the tapestry of my life. I make daily affirmations, visualizing the manifestation of my dreams. With unwavering belief and intentional action, I create a future of abundance and fulfillment."

Carry this affirmation in your heart throughout the day. Let it guide your thoughts and actions. Trust in the power of your mind to shape your reality. By thinking affirmatively, you embark on a transformative journey of self-empowerment and endless possibilities.

V

Loving Wholeheartedly

24

Day 24 Free Your Fears

Fear, the antithesis of love, is the breeding ground for countless negative "isms" that plague our world. Racism stems from the fear of differences and waning dominance. Sexism arises from the fear of emasculation. Insecurity and abuse thrive in the cycle of fear, perpetuating brokenness in individuals and hearts. In simple terms, fear is destructive.

Life's hardships often leave us scarred and develop within us a fear of being hurt again. It is a natural response to pain. Just as a child learns not to touch a hot stove after getting burned, we develop emotional defense mechanisms to protect ourselves. However, this defense mechanism does not serve our emotional well-being. Fear stands in direct opposition to love, hindering our capacity to give and receive love wholeheartedly. To truly love, we must break free from the chains of "what if it happens again?"

Conquering our fears regarding relationships and opportunities demands a mindset of perpetual newness. Once we have forgiven our past, we must approach our future with authority. Each opportunity for love or success is unique, and we must treat it as such. While it is wise to recognize unhealthy patterns and red flags, it is crucial not to view everything through a lens of pessimism. A negative and fearful outlook breeds negative outcomes.

As we encounter negative experiences, especially those that resemble previous ones, we may develop a generalized fear that taints our perception of similar situations. For instance, one bad experience with a dog may lead to a fear of all dogs, assuming that all dogs will harm us. This mental construct restricts us from living an abundant and experiential life. To embrace the fullness of a healed heart, we must understand that life is a connected journey composed of individualized experiences. Each person we meet is unique, each career path holds its own intricacies, and each risk we take will yield distinct results or lessons, even if there are similarities to past experiences. Each day should be embraced with the mindset that it holds newness and the potential for new discoveries, perspectives, and knowledge. Even within the routines, there are hidden gems of novelty waiting to be uncovered. Succumbing to fear will cause us to miss every opportunity for growth and new experiences.

Fear has crippled countless individuals. It keeps people trapped in toxic relationships for fear of losing stability, or prevents them from entering relationships that could uplift and edify them due to the fear of being hurt again. Fear hinders bold career moves and stifles the pursuit of passions. Living in fear is living in bondage.

Our fears do not belong to us alone. They are products of past experiences or upbringing. Whether our fears stem from limited exposure or negative encounters, we must put them into perspective and choose to embrace courage.

Today, I invite you to stand before the mirror and affirm your commitment to free yourself from the bondage of fear:

"I release the grip of fear that has held me captive for far too long. My fears do not define me; they belong to the experiences that shaped them. I choose to embrace courage and step into a life free from the limitations of fear. I will no longer allow fear to dictate my relationships, career choices, or pursuit of my passions. I embrace the uniqueness of each opportunity and approach them with renewed strength and optimism. I am liberated from the shackles of fear, and I walk in the fullness of a healed heart."

Carry this affirmation with you throughout the day. Let it embolden your actions and guide your decisions. Embrace the courage within you and embrace a life free from the chains of fear.

Heart Check:

1. Reflect on a fear that has held you back in your relationships or interactions with others. How has this fear influenced your behavior and choices? How would your relationships be different if you were to release this fear?

2. Consider a fear that has limited your career choices or held you back from pursuing your passions. How has this fear affected your professional growth and fulfillment? What steps can you take to challenge this fear and create a mindset of perpetual newness in your career?

3. Imagine yourself stepping into a future where fear no longer dictates your choices. Visualize the opportunities, relationships, and experiences that await you in this fear-free life. Write a letter to your future self, describing the person you have become and the

achievements you have made by embracing courage and letting go of fear.

25

Day 25 Forgive Your Past

In our journey of healing, it is essential to not only forgive our past childhood experiences but also to extend forgiveness to our adult selves for the mistakes and actions we feel burdened by. Sometimes, it is not childhood pain that haunts us, but rather the choices we made as adults that weigh heavily on our hearts. Building a healthy relationship with both our inner child and our adult self is essential for our healing and growth.

We all make decisions along our life path that we later regret or deem as mistakes. These actions may have caused harm to ourselves or others, or they may have led us astray from the path we envisioned for ourselves. In such moments, it is easy to get trapped in a cycle of guilt, self-blame, and shame. But holding onto these negative emotions only hinders our ability to heal and move forward.

To forgive our adult self, we must recognize that making mistakes is an inherent part of the human experience. None of us are perfect, and we all stumble and falter along the way. These moments do not define our worth or determine our destiny. They are opportunities for growth, self-reflection, and learning.

Start by acknowledging the pain and remorse you feel for the choices you made. Understand that these actions were made from a place of limited knowledge, understanding, or clarity. Embrace the understanding that, in each moment, you were doing the best you could with the resources and awareness you had at that time.

Extend compassion and forgiveness to your adult self, just as you would to a dear friend who made similar mistakes. Recognize that holding onto self-blame and guilt only perpetuates the cycle of negativity and inhibits your ability to move forward and create positive change.

As you stand before the mirror, look into your own eyes and affirm:

"I forgive my past actions and choices as an adult. I release the burden of guilt and shame that weighs on my heart. I acknowledge that I am a human being who is prone to making mistakes. I embrace the lessons and growth that come from these experiences. I extend compassion and forgiveness to my adult self, knowing that I am worthy of love, understanding, and second chances. I choose to heal and move forward with a sense of empowerment and self-acceptance. I am not defined by my mistakes, but by my ability to learn, grow, and transform. I am free to create a future filled with love, authenticity, and purpose."

Carry this affirmation with you throughout the day, and whenever you find yourself dwelling on past actions or feeling burdened by regret, return to this affirmation. Allow it to serve as a reminder that forgiveness is a powerful tool for healing and growth.

Remember, forgiving your adult self is not about dismissing or forgetting your past actions, but about acknowledging them, learning from them, and choosing to move forward with a newfound sense of self-compassion and wisdom. Embrace the journey of self-forgiveness, knowing that it is a vital step towards living a more fulfilling and authentic life.

26

Day 26 Welcome Experience

Experience is the greatest teacher, and life presents us with countless opportunities to learn, grow, and evolve. Each new experience is a precious gift, a chance to expand our horizons, challenge our beliefs, and discover new aspects of ourselves. In this chapter, we will explore the value of welcoming new experiences and how they serve as life's classroom.

When we approach life with an open mind and a willingness to embrace new experiences, we unlock doors to endless possibilities. Every encounter, every adventure, and every interaction becomes an opportunity for personal and spiritual growth. It is through experience that we gain wisdom, develop resilience, and cultivate a deeper understanding of ourselves and the world around us.

Welcome experience as a curious student enters a classroom, ready to absorb knowledge and insights. Recognize that even the seemingly mundane or challenging moments carry valuable lessons. Embrace the uncertainties and step out of your comfort zone, for it is in those moments of discomfort that true transformation occurs.

Each experience offers a unique perspective, allowing us to see life from different angles. It broadens our understanding, deepens our empathy, and nurtures our ability to connect with others. By welcoming diverse experiences, we enrich our own journey and contribute to the collective tapestry of human existence.

As you navigate through the chapters of your life, be mindful of the lessons that each experience brings. Reflect on the growth you have achieved, the resilience you have built, and the wisdom you have gained. Embrace the highs and lows, the victories and setbacks, knowing that they all play a vital role in shaping who you are becoming.

As you stand before the mirror, look into your own eyes and affirm:

"I welcome new experiences into my life with open arms and an open heart. I embrace the unknown and trust that every experience is a valuable teacher. I release the fear of the unfamiliar and step into the classroom of life with curiosity and enthusiasm. I am ready to learn, grow, and evolve. I welcome the lessons that each experience brings, knowing that they contribute to my personal and spiritual growth. I am grateful for the opportunity to expand my horizons and discover new aspects of myself. I embrace the richness and depth that experience offers. Today, I choose to welcome experience as a lifelong student of life."

Carry this affirmation with you throughout the day, and as you encounter new experiences, remind yourself of your willingness to welcome them. Embrace the lessons, the challenges, and the beauty that each moment brings. Trust in the transformative power of experience and the wisdom it imparts.

Remember, life's classroom is ever-present, and the more we welcome experience, the more we open ourselves up to the vast potential that awaits us. Embrace the journey of continuous learning and growth, knowing that every experience is a precious opportunity to become the best version of yourself.

27

Day 27 Own Your Need for Love

In this modern age of technology and instant expressionism, we find ourselves immersed in a world of contrasting images, status updates, and trendy hashtags. Our social media feeds present a mosaic of experiences, ranging from joyous engagements and blissful marriages to defiant selfies with captions proclaiming an eternal commitment to singlehood, adorned with hashtags like #singleforlife. But amidst this digital landscape, we must discern the true meaning behind these posts.

Is it possible that the seemingly effortless allure captured in a #singleforlife photo represents a genuine celebration of independence rather than a shield of jaded loneliness? Perhaps. However, it is crucial to distinguish between embracing solitude out of genuine contentment and accepting it as a result of past disappointments in love and acceptance. Regardless of our individual histories of heartache, every human being possesses an innate desire for companionship and connection. By denying this fundamental need, we deny ourselves a natural aspect of our humanity.

In the timeless words of Nat King Cole, beautifully sung in his rendition of "Nature Boy," he reminds us of a profound truth: "The greatest thing we'll ever learn is just to love and be loved in return." Love is an inherent part of our existence, intricately woven into the fabric of our being. It is not a weakness or a flaw; rather, it is a testament to our capacity for deep connection and vulnerability.

Owning our need for love does not diminish our independence or strength. Instead, it empowers us to acknowledge our innate desire for human connection, reminding us that we are not meant to navigate this world alone. It is an affirmation that we are worthy of love, affection, and belonging. Embracing this truth allows us to cultivate healthy relationships, both with ourselves and with others, fostering an environment of genuine connection and mutual support.

When we own our need for love, we release the self-imposed pressure to conform to societal expectations or to deny our authentic desires. We grant ourselves permission to seek and cultivate meaningful connections, knowing that vulnerability and openness are not signs of weakness, but rather acts of courage and self-love.

So, as you reflect upon your own journey, stand before the mirror and affirm:

"I own my need for love. It is a natural and integral part of my humanity. I embrace my innate desire for companionship and connection, knowing that it does not diminish my independence or strength. I release any shame or fear associated with my need for love, and I open myself up to receive and give love freely. I am deserving of deep, meaningful relationships that nourish my soul and allow me to grow. I honor my authentic desires and embrace the vulnerability that comes with opening my heart. Today, I choose to own my need for love and celebrate the beauty of human connection."

Carry this affirmation with you throughout the day, allowing it to guide your interactions and choices. Embrace the understanding that owning your need for love is a powerful act of self-acceptance and self-care. As you navigate the complexities of relationships and connections, remember that your desire for love is not a weakness but a testament to your resilience and capacity to experience profound joy and fulfillment.

By embracing and owning your need for love, you invite a profound transformation into your life—a transformation that transcends super-ficial appearances and hashtags, and instead embraces the authentic essence of human connection and the transformative power of love.

28

Day 28 Receive Love

Love has an extraordinary ability to manifest in myriad forms, both expected and unexpected. As we continue on this journey, it is essential to cultivate a spirit of openness and receptivity, for love has a way of entering our lives through various channels. It is crucial to recognize that love is not limited to romantic relationships alone; it encompasses a vast spectrum of connections and experiences.

In our quest to receive love, we must first acknowledge the profound truth that love starts from within. It begins with self-acceptance, self-compassion, and self-nurturing. We must learn to cultivate a deep sense of love for ourselves, embracing our flaws and celebrating our unique qualities. When we truly love and accept ourselves, we create a fertile ground for love to flourish in our lives. When I first started doing Mirror Work, I told myself that I desired to be able to look at myself in the mirror the way I would look adoringly at a lover. As a lifelong hopeful romantic, I found myself pouring my ideal of love on people and failing to be deeply in love with self. It was through that mirror work, much like the exercises I've included throughout this book, that I discovered this gateway to loving myself as deeply as I had believed

I loved others. In truth, the love of self will radically empower and invigorate your capacity to love others.

However, love does not only flow from within; it also comes to us through the people and experiences we encounter. Love may be expressed through the unwavering support of a cherished friend, the genuine kindness of a stranger, or the comforting presence of a beloved pet. It may come in the form of a heartfelt letter, a warm embrace, or a simple act of service. Love reveals itself in countless ways, often when we least expect it.

Yet, it is vital to guard against the temptation to confine love within narrow expectations. Love does not always arrive in the exact shape or form we envision. It may not fit the societal ideals or the preconceived notions we hold. In these moments, we must remain open and receptive, allowing love to unfold in its unique and mysterious ways.

By embracing a mindset of openness and receptivity, we free ourselves from the limitations of our expectations. We release the need for love to conform to our rigid definitions, and instead, we embrace its infinite possibilities. Love may come disguised as a lesson, challenging us to grow and evolve. It may arrive as an unexpected connection, teaching us the beauty of human diversity and interconnectedness. Love may even present itself in the face of adversity, guiding us towards resilience and self-discovery.

To receive love, we must cultivate a discerning heart—one that recognizes the genuine intentions and authentic expressions of love, regardless of their packaging. We must be attuned to the whispers of love in our everyday lives, the subtle gestures and moments that carry its essence. We must allow love to touch us deeply, igniting a sense of gratitude and awe for the boundless ways it enriches our existence.

So, as you embark on this day, I encourage you to open your heart and affirm:

"I am open and receptive to love in all its forms. I release the need for love to conform to my expectations and embrace its infinite possibilities. I am worthy of receiving love from within and without. I welcome the connections, experiences, and expressions of love that come my way, knowing that they hold the power to heal. I remain open to the lessons love brings, the growth it nurtures, and the joy it brings. Today, I choose to receive love with gratitude and embrace its boundless manifestations."

Carry this affirmation within you, allowing it to guide your interactions and perceptions. Embrace the wondrous diversity of love and the countless ways it finds its way into your life. Celebrate the beauty of connections, both expected and unexpected, and cherish the transformative power of love in all its forms.

Remember, the act of receiving love is an act of surrender—a surrender to the vastness of love's offerings. As you welcome love with an open heart, you create a sacred space where love can truly thrive and transform your life in ways beyond imagination.

29

Day 29 Value Love: Cherishing the Gift of Love

Love is a precious gift that has the power to enrich our lives in ways beyond measure. It is a force that brings joy, connection, and meaning to our existence. Yet, in the wake of past heartbreaks and disappointments, it is easy to let callouses form around our hearts, shielding us from the vulnerability and excitement that come with cherishing love when it finds us.

As we embark on this journey of healing and growth, it is crucial to recognize the value of love and to not take it for granted. Love is not a guarantee; it is a delicate tapestry woven with care and intention. Each thread represents a unique connection, a shared experience, and a heartfelt exchange. It is a tapestry that can be torn by neglect, indifference, and complacency.

To value love is to approach it with a sense of awe and reverence. It is to recognize the immense privilege of receiving love in our lives and to honor it with gratitude and cherishment. It is a conscious choice to embrace the vulnerability that love requires, even though it may be accompanied by the echoes of past heartbreaks.

When love finds its way to our doorstep, it is a precious opportunity to rewrite our narrative, to break free from the chains of fear and doubt, and to embrace the exhilaration of being cherished and cherished in return. It is a chance to mend the wounds of the past and to allow love to breathe new life into our hearts.

Let us not allow the callouses of past heartbreaks to diminish our capacity to cherish love when it arrives. Instead, let us approach love with a childlike wonder, infused with excitement and hope. Let us savor each moment, relishing in the beauty of shared laughter, gentle touch, and heartfelt conversations. Let us appreciate the simple acts of kindness and affection that fill our days, knowing that they are the building blocks of a love that withstands the test of time.

To value love is to be present in its embrace. It is to set aside the distractions and busyness of life and to fully immerse ourselves in the experience of love. It is to listen with intention, to hold space for vulnerability, and to reciprocate with kindness and compassion. It is to be an active participant in the dance of love, cherishing every step and twirl.

So, as you embark on this day, I encourage you to reflect upon the value of love and affirm:

"I cherish the gift of love in my life. I release the callouses of past heartbreaks and open my heart to the exhilaration of being cherished. I embrace vulnerability, knowing that it is the gateway to deep connection. I am grateful for the simple acts of love that fill my days, and I cherish the shared experiences that enrich my life. Today, I choose to value and honor love, allowing it to shape and transform my existence."

Carry this affirmation within you, allowing it to guide your interactions and perceptions. Cultivate a deep sense of appreciation for the love that graces your life, and let it inspire you to reciprocate with warmth, tenderness, and gratitude. Value love as the precious gift it is, and watch as it unfolds its transformative power in your life.

Remember, to value love is to embrace the vulnerability and excitement that come with cherishing its presence. It is to nurture the flame of love within your heart, allowing it to radiate its warmth and light into the world. Today and every day, let love be your guiding force, and let its value shape the path of your journey.

30

Day 30 Give Love, Embrace the Journey of Healing

Congratulations on reaching the final day of this transformative 30-day journey. It has been a testament to your strength, resilience, and commitment to healing. As we conclude this chapter of our lives, let us delve into the essence of love once more, for it is in giving love relentlessly that we truly find fulfillment.

Throughout these past 30 days, we have explored the depths of our broken hearts, confronted our pain, and embarked on a path of healing. We have learned to forgive, to embrace vulnerability, and to value the love that graces our lives. Now, as we stand at the threshold of a new beginning, we have the opportunity to give love in ways that will reverberate far beyond ourselves.

Giving love begins with ourselves. It is an act of self-compassion and self-acceptance, recognizing our worth and embracing our journey. It is about nurturing our inner child, listening to our needs, and treating ourselves with kindness and grace. By extending love to ourselves, we create a reservoir of abundance that can overflow into the lives of others.

But giving love does not stop at self. It is an expansive force that ripples outward, touching the lives of those around us. It is in the smile we offer to a stranger, the helping hand we lend to a friend in need, and the compassionate ear we lend to someone who is hurting. It is in the acts of generosity, the words of affirmation, and the presence we offer to those we love.

To give love relentlessly is to embody the principles we have explored throughout this journey. It is to forgive even when it feels difficult, to embrace vulnerability even when it scares us, and to value the love that comes our way. It is to choose joy over bitterness, compassion over judgment, and gratitude over entitlement. It is a commitment to being a vessel of love in a world that often yearns for its healing touch.

As we conclude this 30-day journey, I invite you to revisit the principles and insights shared in these pages. Let them serve as a guiding light on your continued path of healing. Understand that healing is not a destination but a lifelong journey. Each person's journey is unique, and it may take twists and turns along the way. But armed with the wisdom and tools we have uncovered, you have the power to navigate your path with grace and resilience.

Remember, healing is not linear. There may be moments when old wounds resurface, when challenges seem insurmountable, and when love feels elusive. In those moments, revisit the days and principles that resonate with you the most. Find solace in the reminders of forgiveness, self-love, and the value of embracing both the joys and pains of life.

You are not alone on this journey. Reach out to your support system, whether it be loved ones, therapists, or community groups. Surround yourself with those who uplift and inspire you, and be a source of support for others as well. Together, we can create a ripple effect of love that spreads far and wide.

As we bid farewell to this 30-day journey, let us carry the spirit of love with us in every step we take. Let us give love relentlessly to ourselves and to others, for it is in the act of giving that we truly receive. May your heart be filled with compassion, your spirit be buoyed by resilience, and your life be a testament to the healing power of love.

Thank you for embarking on this journey with me. May your path be illuminated by love, and may you continue to grow and heal in the embrace of its gentle presence. Farewell, dear friend, but always remember that these words are here for you whenever you need them. Embrace the journey, give love.